EXCLUSIVE SIGNED EDITION

**TANYA BURR**

JUNE 2016

# TANYA BAKES

## TANYA BURR

MICHAEL JOSEPH
*an imprint of*
PENGUIN BOOKS

**With thanks to the following stockists for the photoshoot outfits:**
Pages 10–11: Shirt – Velvet.
Pages 40–41: Jumper – Topshop.
Pages 118–119: Shirt and trousers – Miss Selfridge.
Pages 146–147: Navy cami dress and cardi – Samsoe Samsoe;
Bracelet – PB Jewellery; Rings – Monica Vinader.
Pages 168–169: Cream jumper – Topshop.
Pages 188–189: Shirt – Velvet; Cami – Aloe.
Pages 208–209: Dress – Olivia & Alice.
Jewellery throughout: Monica Viander, PB Jewellery, Maha Lozi, Apples and Figs.

**We are grateful to the following for granting us permission to use their recipes:**
Pages 24–25: Mary Berry's Chocolate Fork Biscuits from *100 Sweet Treats
and Puds* by Mary Berry, published by BBC Books. Reproduced by permission of The Random House Group Ltd.
Pages 144–145: Nigella's Cookie Dough Pots from *Simply Nigella* by Nigella Lawson,
published by Chatto & Windus. Reproduced by permission of The Random House Group Ltd.
Pages 204–205: Jamie Oliver's American Stack Pancakes taken from *Happy Days
with the Naked Chef*.

MICHAEL JOSEPH

UK | USA | Canada | Ireland | Australia | India | New Zealand | South Africa

Michael Joseph is part of the Penguin Random House group of companies
whose addresses can be found at global.penguinrandomhouse.com.

Penguin
Random House
UK

First published 2016
001

Text copyright © Tanya Burr, 2016
Food photography copyright © Susanna Blåvarg, 2016
Portrait copyright © Dan Kennedy, 2016

The moral right of the author has been asserted

All food photography by Susanna Blåvarg.
Photography by Dan Kennedy, pages 10–11, 40–41, 80–81, 118–119, 146–147,
168–169, 188–189, 208–209
Additional photography Tanya Burr

Art directed, designed and set in 11/14pt MT Bell by Smith & Gilmour
Food stylists: Charlie Clapp & Emily Jonzen
Props stylist: Olivia Wardle
Colour reproduction by Rhapsody Ltd, London
Printed and bound in Italy

A CIP catalogue record for this book is available from the British Library

ISBN: 978-1405928991

# CONTENTS

INTRODUCTION 7

# COOKIES & BISCUITS 10

# MUFFINS, CUPCAKES & TRAYBAKES 40

# CAKES & LOAVES 80

# PUDDINGS 118

# PASTRY 146

# BREAD 168

# BRUNCH 188

# SPECIAL OCCASIONS 208

NOTES 244

INDEX 250

ACKNOWLEDGEMENTS 256

# Hi guys

My life has changed a lot over the last few years but one thing that hasn't is my love of baking. I was so overwhelmed with all your positive feedback on the baking chapter of *Love, Tanya* that I decided to write my very own cookbook. And here it is! For many reasons, baking has been really important to me for a long time – ever since I was very little, in fact.

Lots of my happiest childhood memories centre around our family kitchen. It was so much more than a place to eat – it was a place to create, learn, have fun and spend time with the people I love the most. I vividly remember my mum bringing in a chair from the dining room so that I could actually reach the counter. We tried so many different recipes together – she really nurtured my interest in baking. I'm particularly fond of Mary Berry's Chocolate Fork Biscuits, which you'll find on p. 24., because it was our go-to biscuit recipe – so simple but so delicious. I also spent a lot of time in the kitchen with my nanny, who taught me all her tricks and tips. She taught me how to make pastry and I've used the same method ever since. It features in her Apple Pie recipe, which is my all-time favourite and you'll find it on p.150. I am absolutely crazy about this pie – the perfect source of warmth and comfort on those cold, rainy Sundays.

Lots of the recipes in this book have been passed down through my family, some have been shared amongst my friends and some have come about through lots of playing and experimenting in the kitchen. I hope you'll find plenty of tasty treats to share with your friends and family, too.

I'm really not a pro when it comes to baking. For me, it's about being creative and having fun – not being perfect. The only way to learn new techniques and flavour combinations is to try things out. As you guys know if you watch my baking videos, things don't always go to plan but that's just part of the process and it's so much fun when shared with friends. Baking is an activity that we will spend a whole evening doing – just messing about in the kitchen making delicious things to eat while chatting or watching a film. My Cheesecake & Dark Chocolate Cupcakes on p.73 and Millionaires' Shortbread on p.64 are great for sharing. I've also provided a whole chapter of recipes for special occasions, so come Christmas or Halloween, meet up with your friends to make a Festive Yule Log (p.212) or some spooky Skeleton Biscuits (p.225). And for that really special day, see my Ultimate Celebration Cake on p.241 – it's a real showstopper and everyone will love it!

In this book you'll find a variety of recipes – I've aimed to provide something for everyone, however experienced you are in the kitchen. If baking's new to you, start with something from the 'Cookies & Biscuits' or 'Muffins, Cupcakes & Traybakes' chapters. From family favourites like Choc Chip Shortbread (p.15) and Rocky Road (p.49) to something more unusual like my amazing White Chocolate & Nutella Pinwheel Biscuits (p.27), there's plenty to choose from. For those moments when only a cup of tea and piece of cake will do, have a look in

'Cakes & Loaves'. My traditional Cherry Bundt Cake (p.98) is so pretty and satisfying to make, or, for something more indulgent, try the Brownie Cake on p.103 – it's nearly impossible not to have a second slice. I've given you a few pudding recipes because, for me, this is the best part of any meal. Try the Tarte Tatin on p.158 – surprisingly easy and so beautiful, it never fails to impress! Another sure-fire way to amaze your friends and family is with a great pastry-based bake. There's this idea that pastry is super difficult, but give something a go from my 'Pastry' chapter and you'll see that it's so much easier than you think. As is making bread, so check out my 'Bread' chapter for some inspiration. A few years ago, I'd never have imagined that making Pretzels (p.172) or Pizza (p.187) could be so simple. Finally, definitely have a look at my 'Brunch' chapter if, like me, this is your favourite time of day for treating yourself to something homemade. I like nothing better than a lazy weekend morning made even more self-indulgent with some French Toast (p.200) or Jamie Oliver's American Stack Pancakes (p.204). Particularly when you take them back to bed!

For me, baking is a really therapeutic and calming thing to do, whether on my own or with friends and loved ones. It always cheers me up and I hope that by trying out some of the recipes in this book you can share in that happiness. It's always been a dream of mine to have my own bakery somewhere special to me, like Southwold, Walberswick or even London. *Tanya Bakes* is the first step of that journey and I'm so glad to be sharing it with you.

Love, Tanya

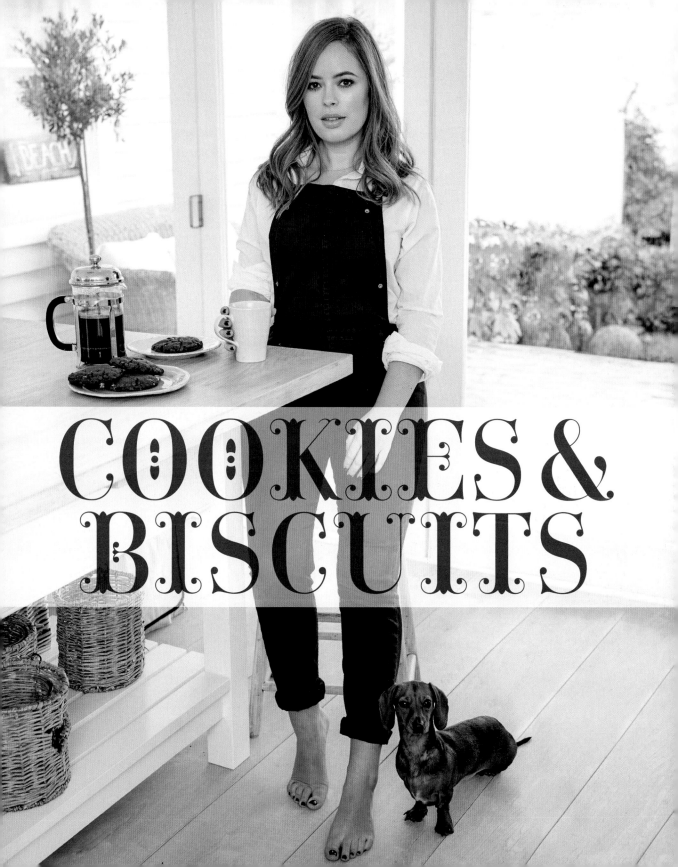

# COOKIES & BISCUITS

# "Make your house smell like a home"

- CHOC CHIP SHORTBREAD
- MINI CHOCOLATE COOKIES
- CRANBERRY, PISTACHIO & CHOCOLATE BISCOTTI
- VANILLA & PISTACHIO BISCUITS
- CUSTARD CREAMS
- MARY BERRY'S CHOCOLATE FORK BISCUITS
- WHITE CHOCOLATE & NUTELLA PINWHEEL BISCUITS
- SALTED NUTELLA COOKIES
- PEANUT BUTTER & DARK CHOCOLATE COOKIES
- CORNFLAKE CHOC CHIP COOKIES
- OAT & CINNAMON HEALTHY COOKIES
- MILK & WHITE CHOCOLATE COOKIES
- TRIPLE CHOCOLATE COOKIES

# CHOC CHIP SHORTBREAD

MAKES ABOUT 15

Prep time: 15 minutes
Cooking time: 20 minutes

Ingredients:
250g plain flour, plus
    extra for dusting
75g caster sugar
175g cold butter
75g milk chocolate chips
75g white chocolate chips
golden caster sugar,
    for sprinkling

I first fell in love with chocolate chip shortbread when I was 17 and working in Starbucks. They used to sell huge triangle pieces of the stuff and I would often have one on my lunchbreak. As you can imagine, the baked goods at Starbucks could never compete with a homemade version, so when I stopped working there I created my own recipe and never looked back.

Preheat the oven to 180°C/350°F/GM4. Line a baking tray with greaseproof paper.

Mix together the flour and sugar, then work the butter in with your fingers until it's the consistency of breadcrumbs.

Add all the chocolate chips, and work the mixture with your hands until a dough is formed – it'll be quite crumbly but should hold its shape when squeezed together.

Roll out the dough on a floured surface to around 1.5cm thick and cut it into fingers, rounds or triangles. Arrange the shortbread onto the tray, leaving some space between each biscuit because they will expand in the oven. Bake for 15–20 minutes or until golden. You might like to neaten the edges of each biscuit while still warm and sprinkle over a little golden caster sugar before transferring them to a wire rack to cool.

# MINI CHOCOLATE COOKIES

MAKES 20-25

Prep time: 20 minutes
Cooking time: 8–10 minutes

Ingredients:
200g unsalted butter,
    softened
300g caster sugar
1 large egg
325g self-raising flour
100g milk chocolate chips
jar of chocolate spread,
    chilled

These cookies are great for when you want some bite-sized treats, their mini-ness makes them super cute and each one is a little mouthful of joy.

Preheat the oven to 180°C/350°F/GM4. Line two baking trays with greaseproof paper.

In a bowl, cream together the butter and sugar until light and fluffy. Add the egg and mix, then add the flour and chocolate chips and combine to form a dough.

Place a small ball of dough in your hand, roughly 2.5cm in diameter. Poke a hole in the middle and spoon in a small amount of chocolate spread – this is easier if the chocolate has been chilled. Cover over the hole with a little more dough, then place on the baking tray and squash down slightly. Repeat with the remaining dough, making sure to leave plenty of space between each ball as they will spread in the oven.

Bake for 8–10 minutes, until golden. Transfer to a wire rack to cool.

# CRANBERRY, PISTACHIO & CHOCOLATE BISCOTTI

MAKES ABOUT 12

Prep time: 15 minutes
Cooking time: 35 minutes

Ingredients:
200g plain flour, plus
   extra to dust
1 teaspoon baking powder
200g caster sugar
100g pistachios, chopped
100g cranberries, chopped
50g dark chocolate, chopped
2 large eggs, beaten
zest of 1 clementine
1 teaspoon vanilla extract

I didn't actually try biscotti until I was about 16, as I would always opt for the gooeyer, more-chocolate-the-merrier treats over an almond biscotti in coffee shops. However, as soon as I tried a homemade version dipped in a hot milky latte, I was converted. Now biscotti have a permanent place in my life. I decided to combine dark chocolate, pistachio and cranberry and it's a winning combination.

Preheat the oven to 180°C/350°F/GM4. Line a baking tray with greaseproof paper.

Put the flour and baking powder into a bowl and add the sugar, pistachios, cranberries and dark chocolate and mix well.

Add the beaten eggs, clementine zest and vanilla extract and mix together to form a dough.

Split the dough in half and shape into two, 5cm-wide cylinders on a floured surface. Place them on a lined baking tray and flatten slightly, leaving space between the two.

Bake for 25–30 minutes until golden.

Allow to cool for 5 minutes, then slice diagonally into 2cm-thick pieces.

Place the biscotti pieces back on the baking tray and return to the oven for 5 minutes. Flip the biscotti over and bake for a further 3 minutes until they are golden and cooked through. Transfer to a wire rack to cool.

# VANILLA & PISTACHIO BISCUITS

MAKES ABOUT 12

Prep time: 15 minutes
Chilling time: 30 minutes
Cooking time: 15 minutes

. . . . . . . . . . . .

Ingredients:
150g unsalted butter, softened
150g light muscovado sugar
pinch of salt
1 teaspoon vanilla bean paste
250g plain flour, plus extra
    for dusting
100g pistachios, half chopped,
    half left whole

These are really cute little biscuits that go perfectly with a cup of tea. When you get to the stage of rolling the dough into a cylinder, you can freeze it. This is great for when you have people coming over spontaneously, as you can simply defrost them and bake them fresh.

. . . . . . . . . . . .

Cream together the butter, sugar, salt and vanilla bean paste.

Work in the flour to form a dough, and fold through all the pistachios at the end.

Halve the dough and roll into 5cm diameter cylinders on a floured surface.

Wrap in clingfilm and chill in the fridge for at least 30 minutes.

When you are ready to bake the biscuits, preheat the oven to 180°C/350°F/GM4. Line a baking tray with greaseproof paper.

Remove the dough from the clingfilm and slice into 1cm-thick rounds.

Place the rounds on the baking tray and bake for 15 minutes until golden. Transfer to a wire rack to cool.

# CUSTARD CREAMS

## MAKES 10

Prep time: 20 minutes
Cooking time: 10 minutes

Ingredients:
100g butter, softened
50g caster sugar
100g plain flour, plus extra
   for dusting
50g custard powder

For the filling:
150g icing sugar
100g butter, softened
a few drops vanilla essence

These traditional biscuits always remind me of my childhood. I would have one with a glass of squash after school. That combination sounds a bit disgusting to me now, though, and I would definitely opt for a cup of tea as my custard cream companion these days! I've invested in an old-fashioned custard cream stamp which I am very fond of, but you can always just pop some dots or a pattern onto your biscuits.

Preheat the oven to 180°C/350°F/GM4. Line a baking tray with greaseproof paper.

In a bowl, cream together the butter and sugar until light and fluffy, then add the flour and custard powder and mix to form a dough.

Roll out the dough on a floured surface to about ½cm thick, then cut into rectangles about 4 x 2.5cm and mark or stamp out with a custard cream cutter. Place on the baking tray. Pop them in the fridge for 10 minutes – the imprint on your biscuits will stay sharper. Bake for 10 minutes, until golden. Transfer to a wire rack to cool.

Whilst the biscuits cool, make the filling. In a bowl, cream together all the filling ingredients until you get a smooth and light icing. When the biscuits are cold, sandwich them together with this filling to form your custard creams.

# MARY BERRY'S CHOCOLATE FORK BISCUITS

## MAKES ABOUT 15

Prep time: 15 minutes
Cooking time: 10–12 minutes

. . . . . . . . . . . . .

Ingredients:
100g unsalted butter,
    softened
50g golden caster sugar
150g self-raising flour,
    plus extra for dusting
25g cocoa powder
splash of milk (optional)

I had to include these biscuits in my baking book as they were the first bake that my sister and I were trusted to make alone whilst our parents watched the news after dinner. We must have made them a hundred times. Mary Berry is one of my biggest baking inspirations.

. . . . . . . . . . . . .

Preheat the oven to 180°C/350°F/GM4. Line a baking tray with greaseproof paper.

In a bowl, cream together the butter and sugar until light and fluffy.

Add the flour and cocoa powder and mix until well combined. Add a splash of milk if the mixture appears too crumbly.

Flour your hands, then roll the dough into 15 small balls. Transfer them to the baking tray and press each ball down with a fork to flatten – it helps to dip the fork in flour.

Bake for 10–12 minutes, then transfer to a wire rack to cool.

# WHITE CHOCOLATE & NUTELLA PINWHEEL BISCUITS

### MAKES 20

Prep time: 20 minutes
Chilling time: 1 hour
Cooking time: 10 minutes

. . . . . . . . . . . .

150g butter, softened
150g caster sugar
1 egg
1 teaspoon vanilla extract
220g plain flour, plus extra
    for dusting
1 teaspoon baking powder
200g Nutella
100g white chocolate, melted

I love these biscuits because they look so impressive but require a lot less effort than you might think. I came up with this recipe one Sunday when Jim was playing on the Xbox (this is when I tend to bake a lot) and when they came out of the oven he was really impressed with how they looked – as well as the yummy Nutella taste. I didn't tell him how I created the pinwheel effect but I guess the secret is out now!

. . . . . . . . . . . .

In a bowl, cream together the butter and sugar until light and fluffy, followed by the egg and vanilla extract.

Stir in the flour and baking powder and mix to form a smooth dough. Split the dough in two. Add Nutella to one half and stir through until well combined. Add the melted white chocolate to the other half and do the same.

Roll out the dough on a floured surface to form two equal rectangles about 1cm thick. Lay out a large piece of clingfilm, then place one rectangle on top of the other. Roll up the whole lot like a Swiss roll, as tightly as possible and wrap in the clingfilm, twisting the ends tightly. Chill in the fridge for 1 hour.

Preheat the oven to 200°C/400°F/GM6. Line a baking tray with greaseproof paper.

Remove the dough from the fridge, unwrap the clingfilm and cut into ½cm discs. Place the discs on the baking tray and bake for 8–10 minutes. Transfer to a wire rack to cool.

# SALTED NUTELLA COOKIES

### MAKES 10

Prep time: 10 minutes
Cooking time: 12 minutes

Ingredients:
200g unsalted butter, softened
300g caster sugar
1 large egg
325 self-raising flour
1 teaspoon flaked sea salt
200g Nutella

Jim and I went to a local café for breakfast and on the way out we eyed up the cookie jars. The guy behind the counter basically forced us (OK, he didn't really) to try one of the cookies (so we bought two). We walked down the street and had a bite each and turned to each other to say OMG. Jim demanded that I go back and ask for the recipe and make a batch that same day. As you can imagine, no little café will give away a secret cookie recipe, so I made up my own and they taste just as good, if not a little better, if I do say so myself!

Preheat the oven to 180°C/350°F/GM4. Line two baking trays with greaseproof paper.

Cream together the butter and sugar until light and fluffy. Mix in the egg until combined, then gradually add the flour and salt until a dough forms. Add the Nutella and gently marble the chocolate through the dough using a wooden spoon or palette knife.

Divide the dough into 10 balls, then squash them down gently onto the baking trays. Make sure to leave plenty of space between each cookie, as they will spread in the oven.

Sprinkle with sea salt, then bake for 12 minutes.

Transfer to a wire rack to cool and set for 20 minutes before eating.

# PEANUT BUTTER & DARK CHOCOLATE COOKIES

MAKES 10

Prep time: 15 minutes
Cooking time: 12 minutes

Ingredients:
175g coconut sugar
125ml coconut oil, melted
1 egg
4 tablespoons smooth
    peanut butter
300g buckwheat flour
½ teaspoon baking powder
pinch of salt
100g dark chocolate (70%
    cocoa solids), chopped
50g raisins

Every now and then I like to experiment with a little 'healthy' baking. Not only for the health reasons, but also for the flavours that some of the ingredients give. Buckwheat flour has an amazing nutty flavour and coconut oil works so well in these cookies. Then if you add three of my favourite things – peanut butter, raisins and dark chocolate – you are on to a winner! I created this recipe with my friend Kate one evening; it was late, all the shops were closed and the boys were demanding cookies and ice-cream, so we kind of just threw together everything that was in the cupboard.

Preheat the oven to 180°C/350°F/GM4. Line two baking trays with greaseproof paper.

Mix the coconut sugar and oil together, then add the egg and peanut butter and mix well.

Add the flour, baking powder and salt and combine to form a cookie batter.

Fold through the chocolate and raisins until well dispersed.

Roll into 10 balls, then flatten each ball onto the baking trays, leaving plenty of space between each cookie, as they will spread in the oven.

Bake for 10–12 minutes, until the cookies are golden. Transfer to a wire rack to cool.

# CORNFLAKE CHOC CHIP COOKIES

## MAKES 12 LARGE COOKIES

Prep time: 15 minutes
Cooking time: 10 minutes

Ingredients:
200g unsalted butter,
    softened
300g golden caster sugar
1 large egg
300g self-raising flour
200g milk chocolate chips
80g cornflakes
pinch of sea salt

These cookies are a happy texture explosion in your mouth! The crunch of the cornflakes with the soft gooey cookie dough is so good, my brother loves it whenever I make cookies, so Oscar this recipe is dedicated to you, please try it out – I think you're going to love it!

Preheat the oven to 200°C/400°F/GM6. Line two baking trays with greaseproof paper.

Cream together the butter and sugar until light and fluffy, then whisk in the egg until smooth.

Add the flour, chocolate chips, cornflakes and sea salt to form a dough. Divide into 12 balls.

Squash the balls down onto the baking tray leaving plenty of space between each cookie, as they will spread in the oven.

Bake for 10–12 minutes, until the cookies are golden. Transfer to a wire rack to cool.

# OAT & CINNAMON HEALTHY COOKIES

## MAKES 20

Prep time: 15 minutes
Cooking time: 15–20 minutes

Ingredients:
300g oats
100g butter, softened
1 teaspoon baking powder
1 egg
3 tablespoons honey
2 teaspoons ground
    cinnamon
large handful of raisins

As far as cookies go, these are actually pretty good for you. They make a really easy on-the-go breakfast or snack.

Preheat the oven to 180°C/350°F/GM4. Line two baking trays with greaseproof paper.

Put all the ingredients apart from the raisins into a bowl and mix to form a dough. Add the raisins and mix through until well dispersed.

Form the dough into 20 balls, then press them gently onto the baking trays to form a cookie shape, spacing them apart, as they will spread in the oven.

Bake in the oven for 15–20 minutes, until golden and crisp. Transfer to a wire rack to cool.

# MILK & WHITE CHOCOLATE COOKIES

MAKES 10

Prep time: 15 minutes
Cooking time: 12 minutes

Ingredients:
200g white chocolate
200g milk chocolate
200g unsalted butter,
    softened
300g caster sugar
1 large egg
325g self-raising flour
vanilla ice-cream, for
    sandwiching (optional)

I had to include my milk and white chocolate cookie recipe from my first book *Love, Tanya* as everyone seemed to love it so much. You can put a twist on it this recipe if you like and make one of my favourite things ever, ice-cream cookie sandwiches. I remember eating an ice-cream cookie sandwich whilst walking along New York's Highline in the sunshine sharing it with a friend, so this recipe reminds me of that happy time.

Preheat the oven to 180°C/350°F/GM4. Line two baking trays with greaseproof paper.

Using a knife, cut all the chocolate into small chunks and set aside.

In a bowl, cream together the butter and sugar until pale and fluffy. Add the egg and beat until smooth.

Gradually add the flour until well combined, then add the chocolate chunks.

Divide into 10 balls and squash them down gently onto the baking trays. Remember that they'll spread in the oven, so be sure to leave plenty of space between each cookie.

Bake for 12 minutes. They'll still be very gooey, but don't worry – they'll set as they cool down. Transfer to a wire rack to cool.

To make ice-cream sandwiches, spread some ice-cream onto one cold cookie, then place another cold cookie directly on top.

# TRIPLE CHOCOLATE COOKIES

MAKES 10 VERY LARGE COOKIES

Prep time: 15 minutes
Cooking time: 11 minutes

Ingredients:
200g unsalted butter, softened
300g caster sugar
1 large egg
275g self-raising flour
75g cocoa powder
a dash of milk (optional)
100g each of white, milk
    and dark chocolate
3 Dime (Daim) bars

I originally baked these cookies and shared the recipe on my YouTube channel because I was inspired by a video I had seen online about how to make 'Ben's Cookies'. For any of you who haven't tried Ben's Cookies, it's a chain found all over London, and across the world as far as Seoul, which sells incredible cookies. They have a crunch on the outside and are super gooey on the inside. I played around with the recipe a bit and added Dime/Daim bars to the mix (although I've been known to add whatever chocolate we have in the cupboard – Rolos work great!). These are seriously the most delicious cookies you will ever eat. I'll always whip up a batch when I have friends and family coming over as they all love them and it makes the house smell amazing, too!

Preheat your oven to 200°C/400°F/GM6. Line two trays with greaseproof paper.

Cream together the butter and sugar, then crack in the egg and beat until smooth.

Add the dry ingredients – plus a splash of milk if it's looking too dry.

Break up the chocolate and add to the mixture.

Divide the dough into 10 balls, then squash them gently onto the baking trays. Remember that the cookies will spread, so leave plenty of space between each ball.

Bake for 11 minutes. Transfer to a wire rack to cool.

# MUFFINS, CUPCAKES & TRAYBAKES

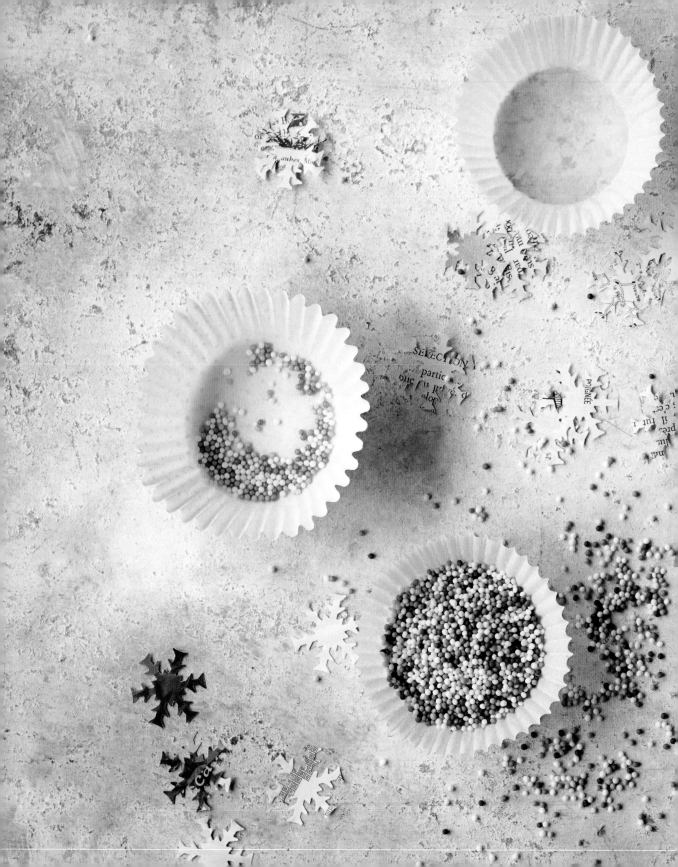

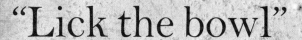

# "Lick the bowl"

RASPBERRY & LEMON FRIANDS

PEACHES & CREAM MUFFINS

ROCKY ROAD

BLUEBERRY MUFFINS

RASPBERRY CUPCAKES

PEANUT BUTTER CUPS

SALTED CARAMEL BROWNIES

CHOCOLATE HONEYCOMB CARAMEL CUPCAKES

RHUBARB & CUSTARD MUFFINS

S'MORES CUPCAKES

MILLIONAIRES' SHORTBREAD

KATE'S MUM'S LEMON SLICE

SMARTIES FLAPJACKS

PUMPKIN WHOOPIE PIES

CHEESECAKE & DARK CHOCOLATE CUPCAKES

AMAZING CHOCOLATE BROWNIES

MARSHMALLOW RICE KRISPIE SQUARES

VANILLA STAR-SPRINKLED CUPCAKES

# RASPBERRY & LEMON FRIENDS

MAKES 8

Prep time: 15 minutes
Cooking time: 20 minutes

*You will need a 9-hole
cupcake/muffin tray*

Ingredients:
150g butter, melted
 and cooled, plus extra
 for greasing
4 egg whites
100g ground almonds
50g plain flour
175g icing sugar, plus
 extra for dusting
zest of 1 lemon
150g raspberries

To decorate:
flaked almonds

These adorable little friands are perfect for any occasion. They are wonderfully light and the almond and fruit flavours are yummy.

Preheat the oven to 180°C/350°F/GM4. Generously grease 8 holes of the cupcake/muffin tray.

Whisk the egg whites in a clean dry bowl until they are white and frothy, then fold in the ground almonds, flour, icing sugar, most of the zest and the butter to make a smooth batter, being careful to knock out as little air as possible.

Divide the batter between the eight holes and pop three raspberries on top of each. Bake for 20 minutes until golden and risen. Transfer to a wire rack to cool.

Dust with extra icing sugar, the rest of the lemon zest and a sprinkling of flaked almonds.

# PEACHES & CREAM MUFFINS

MAKES 12 MUFFINS

Prep time: 20 minutes
Cooking time: 25 minutes

*You will need a 12-hole cupcake/muffin tray*

Ingredients:
300g peaches, chopped,
   reserve 24 slices
   to decorate
1½ tablespoons caster sugar
150g light brown soft sugar
30ml vegetable oil
1 egg
300ml buttermilk
300g self-raising flour, sifted
1 teaspoon ground cinnamon
300ml double cream

These light and fluffy muffins filled with fresh peaches are one of my favourite creations. I wanted to include cream somehow for that classic peaches and cream combination. At first I tried putting cream into the mixture but you couldn't really taste it once the muffins were cooked, so I then decided to fill the muffins with cream at a later stage. They are just delightful!

Preheat the oven to 200°C/400°F/GM6.

Slice the peaches, place on a baking tray and sprinkle with the caster sugar. Roast for 15 minutes until syrupy and tender, then set aside to cool.

Reduce the oven temperature to 180°C/350°F/GM4 and line the cupcake/muffin tray with paper cases.

Whisk together the light brown sugar, oil, egg and buttermilk until well combined, then fold in the sifted flour and cinnamon. Add the peaches and stir to evenly distributed.

Spoon the batter into the muffin cases and bake for 25 minutes until risen and golden. You can check whether they're cooked through by inserting a skewer into a muffin. If it comes out clean, they're ready. Transfer to a wire rack to cool.

Meanwhile, whisk the double cream until it reaches a thick piping consistency. Poke a good-sized hole in the top of each muffin using a skewer and, using a piping bag or spoon, add a generous dollop of thick cream into each hole before topping with the reserved peach slices.

# ROCKY ROAD

SERVES 8-10

Prep time: 15 minutes
Chilling time: at least 2 hours

*You will need a 20cm
square baking tin*

Ingredients:
150g butter
350g dark chocolate
    (70% cocoa solids)
4 tablespoons golden syrup
250g Maryland cookies
    (or your favourite)
150g mini marshmallows
icing sugar, to dust

These are my Rocky Roads. I have already shared this recipe with you on my YouTube channel but of course I had to include it here as well. This recipe couldn't be easier but the results are great. Feel free to add your own twists, like putting in whatever biscuits you have in the cupboard.

Line a 20cm square baking tin with greaseproof paper.

Melt the butter, chocolate and syrup together in a saucepan on a low heat.

Put the cookies into a ziplock bag and bash with a rolling pin until you have a mixture of big chunks and crumbs.

Pour the crushed cookies into the chocolate mixture and stir in the marshmallows.

Pour the mixture into the tin, cover with clingfilm and transfer to the fridge to set for a minimum of 2 hours.

Remove from the fridge, turn upside down onto a plate and peel off the greaseproof paper. Dust with icing sugar and cut into bars.

These are such a classic, requested by my husband Jim. There's nothing better than biting into a fresh blueberry muffin and seeing the beautiful plump blue fruit inside.

# BLUEBERRY MUFFINS

MAKES 12

Prep time: 15 minutes
Cooking time: 20–25 minutes

*You will need a 12-hole cupcake/muffin tray*

Ingredients:
1 egg
30ml vegetable oil
70g light brown soft sugar, plus extra for sprinkling
300ml buttermilk
300g self-raising flour, sifted
200g punnet of blueberries

Preheat the oven to 180°C/350°F/GM4. Line the cupcake/muffin tray with paper cases.

Mix together the egg, oil, sugar and buttermilk, then fold in the sifted flour until you have a smooth batter.

Gently fold in the blueberries, then divide the mixture between the cases.

Bake for 20–25 minutes until they're risen and golden.

Sprinkle with extra sugar while still hot, then transfer to a wire rack to cool.

# RASPBERRY CUPCAKES

## MAKES 12

Prep time: 20 minutes
Cooking time: 20 minutes

*You will need a 12-hole cupcake/muffin tray*

Ingredients:
50g butter, softened
180g caster sugar
1 egg
splash of vanilla extract
160g plain flour
2 teaspoons baking powder
160ml full-fat milk
raspberry jam, for the filling

For the icing:
250g butter, softened
500g icing sugar
½ teaspoon vanilla extract
pink food colouring

To decorate:
raspberries and edible
    gold glitter

These are really simple, elegant and scrumptious cupcakes. The jammy centre makes them extra moist inside and they look so pretty as part of an afternoon tea spread.

Preheat the oven to 180°C/350°F/GM4. Line the cupcake/muffin tray with paper cases.

Cream together the butter and sugar until light and fluffy. Mix in the egg and vanilla extract, then fold in the flour and baking powder. Slowly add the milk until you have a smooth batter.

Spoon the mixture into the cupcake cases and bake for 18–20 minutes. Transfer to a wire rack to cool.

Once cool, cut out a hole in the middle of each cupcake and spoon in enough raspberry jam to fill each hole.

For the icing, in a bowl cream the butter and carefully add the icing sugar until well incorporated. Mix until light and smooth, then add the vanilla extract and a few drops of food colouring to make a pink icing.

Pipe the icing onto the cupcakes, then top each one with a raspberry dipped in edible gold glitter.

# PEANUT BUTTER CUPS

MAKES 8

Prep time: 20 minutes
Chilling time: 20 minutes

*You will need a 9-hole cupcake/muffin tray*

Ingredients:
200g dark chocolate
   (70% cocoa solids)
3 tablespoons coconut oil
100g smooth peanut butter
4 tablespoons ground almonds
1 tablespoon maple syrup
pinch of sea salt

To decorate (optional):
a few flakes of sea salt
chopped peanuts

When I first moved to London, I lived right by an LA-style health café and became addicted to their peanut butter cups. I ended up feeling that because I made the trip to go there a bit too often specifically for the peanut butter cups, I should try to make them at home. There was no chance they would reveal their golden recipe (believe me, I tried) so I had to resort to guesswork, which is all part of the fun anyway!

Line the cupcake/muffin tray with 8 paper cases – gold foil for the best look.

Melt the chocolate and coconut oil in a bowl placed over a pan of boiling water, making sure the bottom of the bowl does not touch the water. Spoon 1½ tablespoons of the mixture into each cupcake case, then set aside to cool slightly.

Mix together the peanut butter, ground almonds, maple syrup and salt in a small bowl. Roll the mixture into eight balls, then flatten them with your hands to fit into each case on top of the chocolate.

Spoon the remaining melted chocolate into each case so that the peanut butter is covered.

Sprinkle with a few sea salt flakes, or even chopped peanuts, if you like, then transfer to the fridge to chill and set for at least 20 minutes before serving.

# SALTED CARAMEL BROWNIES

### MAKES 16-20

Prep time: 15 minutes
Cooking time: 25 minutes

*You will need a 30 × 20cm baking tin*

Ingredients:
200g butter
300g dark chocolate (70% cocoa solids), chopped
300g golden caster sugar
4 eggs
1 teaspoon vanilla extract
160g plain flour
60g cocoa powder
1 tin Carnation caramel
1 teaspoon sea salt flakes

The combination of chocolate and salted caramel makes for the best partners in crime. These brownies are mouthwateringly luscious. I love to eat them in the afternoon with a cup of tea or warm them in the oven and serve them alongside salted caramel ice-cream for pudding. Trust me, this will become your staple brownie recipe!

Preheat the oven to 180°C/350°F/GM4. Line the baking tin with greaseproof paper.

Melt the butter and dark chocolate in a bowl set over a pan of simmering water, making sure the bottom of the bowl is not touching the water.

Remove the bowl from the pan. Whisk the sugar into the melted chocolate and butter, then add the eggs and vanilla extract and whisk well until light and bubbly.

Carefully fold in the flour and cocoa powder, trying to knock out as little air as possible.

Pour half of the mixture into the baking tin, then pour over the tin of caramel, spread evenly and sprinkle with the sea salt flakes. Pour over the remaining chocolate mixture and bake for 20–25 minutes. Don't worry if it has a slight wobble – it will continue to cook as it cools and will become nice and fudgy.

Allow to cool completely in the tin, then turn out and cut into squares.

# CHOCOLATE HONEYCOMB CARAMEL CUPCAKES

### MAKES 12

Prep time: 25 minutes
Cooking time: 20 minutes

*You will need a 12-hole cupcake/muffin tray*

Ingredients:
50g butter, softened
180g caster sugar
1 egg
splash of vanilla extract
100g plain flour
60g cocoa powder
2 teaspoons baking powder
160ml full-fat milk
100g milk chocolate chips

For the icing:
500g icing sugar
250g butter, softened
200g caramel

To decorate:
2 Crunchie bars

These cupcakes are inspired by one of my favourite chocolate bars, the Crunchie. I also hope these will convert my dad to cupcakes as honeycomb is one of his favourite foods, but he's not the biggest cupcake fan. So, Dad, please make these the first things you bake from my book!

Preheat the oven to 180°C/350°F/GM4. Line the cupcake/muffin tray with paper cases.

In a bowl, cream together the butter and sugar until light and fluffy. Stir in the egg and vanilla, then fold in the flour, cocoa powder and baking powder. Slowly add the milk to form a smooth batter then stir in the chocolate chips. Spoon the mixture evenly into the cupcake cases.

Bake in the oven for 20 minutes, then transfer to a wire rack to cool.

For the icing, mix together all the ingredients until smooth and spoon or pipe onto the cupcakes. Chop up the Crunchie bars into rough pieces and sprinkle on top of each cupcake.

# RHUBARB & CUSTARD MUFFINS

## MAKES 12

Prep time: 20 minutes
Cooking time: 25 minutes

· · · · · · · · · · · · ·

*You will need a 12-hole cupcake/muffin tray*

Ingredients:
300g rhubarb
35g caster sugar
300g self-raising flour
150g light brown soft sugar
1 teaspoon vanilla extract
200ml buttermilk
1 egg
2 tablespoons vegetable oil
100ml ready-made custard

When I came up with the idea for a rhubarb and custard muffin I was so excited. Rhubarb crumble with custard is one of my all-time favourite puddings, so to take those flavours and put them inside a soft pillowy muffin was a no-brainer!

· · · · · · · · · · · · ·

Preheat the oven to 180°C/350°F/GM4. Line the cupcake/muffin tray with paper cases.

Wash and chop the rhubarb into chunky pieces, then arrange in a shallow dish and cover with the caster sugar. Set aside to macerate for 15 minutes.

Mix together the flour and sugar, then add the vanilla extract, buttermilk, egg and vegetable oil and combine to form a smooth batter. Add the rhubarb, reserving 12 pieces to decorate, and fold through the mixture.

Divide half of the batter between the muffin cases, then top each one with a spoonful of custard. Carefully add the remaining batter to each case to cover the custard, then pop a rhubarb piece on top of each muffin.

Bake for 25 minutes until risen and golden. Transfer to a wire rack to cool.

# S'MORES CUPCAKES

MAKES 12

Prep time: 40 minutes
Cooking time: 22 minutes

*You will need a 12-hole cupcake/muffin tray*

Ingredients:
250g digestive biscuits
175g unsalted butter
180g caster sugar
1 egg
splash of vanilla extract
160ml milk
1 big bar (200g) Cadbury's
    milk chocolate

For the fudge icing:
250g salted butter, softened
275g icing sugar
1 teaspoon vanilla extract
200g dark chocolate
    (70% cocoa solids)

For the marshmallow icing:
4 tablespoons golden syrup
150g mini white marshmallows

To decorate:
12 pieces chunky milk
    chocolate

A staple campfire favourite in the US, this has increasingly become a favourite for us Brits, too, over the past few years. I thought it would be a fun idea to make some deconstructed S'mores cupcakes. The Americans use Graham crackers but as they aren't easy to get here, I've opted for digestive biscuits, but you could use Rich Tea biscuits, if you prefer.

Preheat the oven to 180°C/350°F/GM4. Line the cupcake/muffin tray with paper cases.

Crumb the digestives in a processor or crush them with a rolling pin. Melt 125g of the butter, add it to the biscuits and mix thoroughly. Divide the digestive mix between the paper cases, then squash down firmly with your fingers so it lines the base of each case. Set aside.

For the batter, cream together the remaining 50g butter and the caster sugar until light and fluffy. Add the egg and vanilla extract, then fold in the flour and baking powder. Slowly add the milk and mix until smooth and well combined.

Divide the mixture between the cases, then press a square of chocolate into each. Bake for 20 minutes until golden and risen. Transfer to a wire rack to cool.

For the fudge icing, combine the butter, icing sugar and vanilla extract until smooth. Melt the chocolate in a bowl over a pan of simmering water, making sure the bottom of the bowl doesn't touch the water. Stir the chocolate through the icing mixture. Using a piping bag or spoon, pipe the icing on top of the cupcake.

For the marshmallow icing, melt the marshmallows and golden syrup in a pan over a medium heat and stir together. Transfer to a piping bag and allow to cool slightly before piping on top of the fudge icing.

Cool and set the piped marshmallow then flash under a very hot, preheated grill for a minute until golden brown. Add a square of chocolate to the top of each.

# MILLIONAIRES' SHORTBREAD

MAKES 12–15 SQUARES

Prep time: 30 minutes
Cooking time: 20 minutes
Setting time: 20 minutes

*You will need a 20cm square baking tin*

Ingredients:
175g cold butter
250g plain flour
75g caster sugar

For the caramel:
100g butter
100g golden caster sugar
2 tablespoons golden syrup
1 tin (379g) condensed milk

For the topping:
350g milk chocolate
gold edible glitter (optional)

When I was 14, I worked in a little farm shop selling fruit, vegetables and locally baked goods. We were allowed to eat whatever we liked whilst working, as long as we wrote it down in a little book so that it could be taken off our wages at the end of the month. The notebook would read something along the lines of 'Sarah: 1 carrot, Tanya: 5 millionaires' shortbreads'. I love them!

Preheat the oven to 180°C/350°F/GM4. Line a 20cm square baking tin with greaseproof paper.

To make the shortbread, rub the butter in to the flour and sugar until you have a breadcrumb consistency. Knead the mixture together, then press it tightly into the bottom of the tin.

Bake in the oven for 20 minutes until golden, then leave to cool completely.

For the caramel, melt together the butter, sugar, golden syrup and condensed milk in a pan over a medium heat. Bring to the boil, all the while stirring, until the mixture has thickened slightly and turned a light golden colour.

Pour the caramel over the shortbread, spread it out evenly and leave to cool.

When the caramel is cool, make the chocolate topping. Melt the chocolate in a bowl set over a pan of simmering water, making sure the bottom of the bowl isn't touching the water. Pour on top of the caramel and spread evenly.

Allow to cool and set, then sprinkle with edible gold glitter, if using, and cut into squares.

# KATE'S MUM'S LEMON SLICE

### SERVES 10-12

Prep time: 15 minutes
Chilling time: at least
2 hours

............

*You will need a 20cm square baking tin*

Ingredients:
375g digestive biscuits
   (roughly ¾ of a packet)
170g butter, softened
1 tin (370g) condensed milk
225g desiccated coconut,
zest and juice of 2 lemons

For the topping:
225g icing sugar
50g butter, melted
juice of 1 lemon

To decorate:
coconut shavings

My friend Kate and I have been best friends for 12 years, that's 12 years of fun, laughter and her mum Wendy's lemon slices. They are something that she often brings out on a summer's afternoon post-barbecue and they are gone in seconds. I called Wendy to ask if I could if I could share her secret recipe in my book and she said yes. This really is your lucky day! It's hard to compare these slices to anything else, as there's nothing quite like them. The sharp lemon with the sweet coconut and biscuit is really exquisite.

............

Line a 20cm square baking tin with greaseproof paper.

Crush the biscuits then mix together with all the base ingredients and pour into a square tin. Even out and press down the mixture with a metal spoon, making sure it's level.

To make the topping, mix together all the ingredients until you have quite a thick, spreadable paste. If it looks too runny, add more icing sugar.

Spread over the top of the base and sprinkle with some coconut shavings

Transfer to the fridge and chill for at least 2 hours, or until firm.

Once chilled, place a chopping board over the tin and turn upside down. Remove the greaseproof paper, turn it back again onto a serving plate, cut into slices and serve.

# SMARTIES FLAPJACKS

MAKES 9

Prep time: 10 minutes
Cooking time: 20 minutes

*You will need a 20cm square baking tin*

Ingredients:
125g butter
10 tablespoons golden syrup
100g light soft brown sugar
250g porridge oats
1 tube Smarties

Flapjacks are something I've always made growing up and they remind me of my piano teacher, Mrs Fisher. Before my lessons, she had always been baking and sometimes I would arrive an hour before my piano lesson to eat her flapjacks and play with the other children who were there. These are my own chocolatey take!

Preheat the oven to 180°C/350°F/GM4. Line a 20cm square baking tin with greaseproof paper.

Melt the butter in a medium pan over a low heat, then add the golden syrup and sugar. Heat gently until the sugar has dissolved and stir until everything is well combined.

Remove from the heat and stir in the oats. Mix until well combined.

Pour into the tin, spread and squash down with a metal spoon, then bake in the oven for 20 minutes.

While still hot, press the Smarties into the top. Leave to cool in the tin. Once cool, cut into squares.

# PUMPKIN WHOOPIE PIES

MAKES 10

Prep time: 25 minutes
Cooking time: 15 minutes

Ingredients:
420g plain flour
1 teaspoon salt
1 teaspoon baking powder
1 teaspoon bicarbonate of soda
1 tablespoon ground ginger
340g soft light brown sugar
225ml vegetable oil
1 tin (424g) pumpkin purée
2 eggs
1 teaspoon vanilla paste

For the filling:
200g butter, softened
500g icing sugar
1 teaspoon vanilla paste
300g full-fat cream cheese

I love how fun these scrumptious whoopie pies look. Sweet cream cheese filling sandwiched between two soft dome-shaped pumpkin cakes. I love the colour that the pumpkin gives and also, whilst making them, the smell of the pumpkin purée always takes me back to carving pumpkins on Halloween.

Preheat the oven to 180°C/350°F/GM4. Line two baking trays with greaseproof paper.

Put all the dry ingredients, minus the sugar, in a large bowl and mix.

In another bowl, whisk together the sugar and oil until well combined, then add the pumpkin purée, eggs and vanilla and whisk again until smooth.

Pour the wet ingredients into the dry ingredients and combine.

Using a small ice-cream scoop with a release, scoop balls of dough and space them apart on the baking tray.

Bake for 15 minutes until golden, then transfer to a wire rack to cool.

Make the filling by creaming the butter in a bowl and slowly adding the icing sugar and vanilla paste until fully incorporated and smooth. Stir through the cream cheese until smooth – you might need to pop it in the fridge for 5 minutes as stirring cream cheese can sometimes make it watery.

Sandwich the cookies together with a thick layer of cream cheese filling and enjoy!

# CHEESECAKE & DARK CHOCOLATE CUPCAKES

## MAKES 12

Prep time: 30 minutes
Cooking time: 20 minutes

. . . . . . . . . . . .

*You will need a 12-hole cupcake/muffin tray*

Ingredients:
50g butter, softened
180g caster sugar
1 egg
splash of vanilla extract
60g cocoa powder
100g plain flour
2 teaspoons baking powder
50g milk chocolate chips
160ml milk

For the filling:
250g cream cheese
100g caster sugar
2 large eggs
1 teaspoon sea salt
1 teaspoon vanilla extract
50g dark chocolate chips

For the icing:
500g icing sugar
250g slightly salted butter, softened
½ teaspoon vanilla extract

To decorate:
chocolate shavings

A few years ago, before I moved to London and when I was just a tourist in the Big City, I discovered the Hummingbird bakery. They are famous for their black-bottom cupcakes – amongst so many other amazing bakes – but this is the one that Jim and I would always go for. Living so far from the nearest Hummingbird bakery whilst I was in Norwich, I tried making them myself at home and after a few goes, this is what I came up with.

. . . . . . . . . . . .

Preheat the oven to 180°C/350°F/GM4. Line the cupcake/muffin tray with paper cases.

Make the cheesecake filling by mixing together the cream cheese and caster sugar in a bowl. Add in the eggs, one at a time. Stir in the salt, vanilla and dark chocolate chips, then set aside.

For the cupcakes, in a bowl cream together the butter and caster sugar until light and fluffy. Mix in the egg and vanilla extract, then fold in the cocoa powder, flour, baking powder and milk chocolate chips and add the milk to form a smooth batter.

Put a tablespoon of the cheesecake filling into each cupcake case, followed by the chocolate batter, until they are three-quarters full. Bake for 20 minutes then transfer to a wire rack to cool.

Make the icing by combining all the ingredients until smooth. Pipe onto the cooled cupcakes and decorate with chocolate shavings.

# AMAZING CHOCOLATE BROWNIES

MAKES 12–16

Prep time: 15 minutes
Cooking time: 30 minutes

. . . . . . . . . . . . . .

*You will need a 20cm square baking tin*

Ingredients:
125ml coconut oil
300g dark chocolate
    (70% cocoa solids), plus
    extra melted, for drizzling
400g coconut sugar
170g ground almonds
1 teaspoon baking powder
½ avocado, mashed
½ teaspoon vanilla extract
pinch of salt
3 eggs

These brownies contain different ingredients to traditional brownies, but don't compromise on taste or texture. They are great for those of you with dairy and wheat intolerances. I actually prefer this recipe to any traditional brownie recipe; it took a lot of attempts to get it right and I am so thankful for my guinea pig, Jim, who ate brownies until they were coming out of his ears for about a week! It was so worth it once I got them right, though, and now I make them all the time. Jim made these the other day and asked me if I thought it would be a good idea to add a large tablespoon of peanut butter to the mixture, so I said go for it. This would be a great addition for any of you peanut-butter lovers.

. . . . . . . . . . . .

Preheat the oven to 180°C/350°F/GM4. Line a 20cm square baking tin with greaseproof paper.

In a large saucepan, heat the coconut oil and chocolate, stirring, over a low heat, until melted.

Turn off the heat, add the remaining ingredients, then mix until fully combined.

Pour into the baking tin and bake for 30 minutes. Leave to cool in the tin before drizzling with the melted chocolate and then cutting and eating.

# MARSHMALLOW RICE KRISPIE SQUARES

MAKES 12-15

As you can probably tell from reading this book, I am such a sentimental person, I really wanted every bake I put in here to remind me of a certain day, memory or moment. Marshmallow Rice Krispie Squares were all the rage when I was at school. Our school chef made them in all different flavours, sometimes with melted chocolate on top. I have to say I love the original, so that's what I have created here.

Prep time: 10 minutes
Setting time: 30 minutes

*You will need a 30 × 20cm baking tin*

50g salted butter
300g mini marshmallows, plus a handful for decoration
150g Rice Krispies

Line a 30 x 20cm baking tin with greaseproof paper.

Melt the butter in a saucepan over a medium heat.

Tip in the marshmallows and stir constantly until they're melted and smooth.

Take off the heat and stir in the Rice Krispies. Mix with a spatula until well combined.

Pour the mixture into the tin and spread it out evenly. Scatter over a handful of marshmallows for decoration. Allow to cool completely before cutting into squares.

# VANILLA STAR-SPRINKLED CUPCAKES

## MAKES 12 CUPCAKES

Prep time: 20 minutes
Cooking time: 15–20 minutes

. . . . . . . . . . . . .

*You will need a 12-hole cupcake/muffin tray*

Ingredients:
50g unsalted butter, softened
180g caster sugar
1 egg
1 teaspoon vanilla extract
160g plain flour
2 teaspoons baking powder
160ml milk

For the icing:
500g icing sugar
250g unsalted butter,
    softened
½ teaspoon vanilla extract

To decorate (optional):
chocolate stars and
    glitter sprinkles

These were some of the first cakes I made when I was little, with my mum. We used to call them fairy cakes as this was about 20 years before the cupcake craze began! They are pretty, cute and yummy, too, they will not fail to put a smile on anyone's face.

. . . . . . . . . . . . .

Preheat the oven to 180°C/350°F/GM4. Line the cupcake/muffin tray with paper cases.

In a bowl, cream together the butter and sugar until light and fluffy, then mix in the egg and vanilla extract.

Fold in the flour and baking powder, then slowly add the milk, beating as you go until you have a smooth batter.

Spoon the mixture evenly into the cupcake cases and bake for 15–20 minutes until golden. Transfer to a wire rack to cool.

For the icing, mix together all the ingredients until smooth. Spoon or pipe onto the cupcakes and decorate with chocolate stars and glitter, or whatever you fancy.

# CAKES & LOAVES

# "Time for a spot of afternoon tea"

CAPPUCCINO CAKE

SUNDAY CAKE

EARL GREY TEA LOAF

CHOCOLATE LOAF

LEMON DRIZZLE LOAF

PISTACHIO CAKE WITH LEMON CURD

MOCHA CAKE

CHERRY BUNDT CAKE

FLOURLESS COCONUT & LIME CAKE

BROWNIE CAKE

CARROT CAKE

RAINBOW CAKE

AUSTRALIAN TOASTED BANANA BREAD

PLUM & ALMOND CAKE

GINGERBREAD LOAF

VICTORIA SPONGE CAKE

SUPER DUPER CHOCOLATE CAKE

# CAPPUCCINO
# CAKE

### SERVES 8-10

Prep time: 20 minutes
Cooking time: 20 minutes

*You will need 2 × 21cm round
loose-bottomed cake tins*

Ingredients:
225g butter, softened
225g light soft brown sugar
4 eggs
150ml strong coffee, cooled
250g self-raising flour

For the icing:
150g butter, softened
300g icing sugar
2 teaspoons instant coffee,
   mixed with 3 tablespoons
   hot water

cocoa powder, for dusting
   (optional)

Ever since I was a little girl I have loved the taste of
coffee. Coffee-flavoured chocolates, coffee-flavoured
ice cream and, of course, coffee-flavoured cake have
always been something I would choose. So I came
up with this cappuccino cake recipe especially for
this book. The cake is moist and light and the icing
is top notch.

Preheat the oven to 180°C/350°F/GM4. Line
the cake tins with greaseproof paper.

In a bowl, cream together the butter and sugar,
then mix in the eggs and coffee. Stir in the flour
to form a smooth batter.

Divide between the two tins and bake for 20 minutes
until golden and springy. Cool a little in the tins then
transfer to a wire rack to cool completely.

Make the icing by mixing together the butter and
sugar in a bowl until pale and smooth. Stir in the
coffee and mix again until well combined.

Using a palette knife, sandwich the two cakes
together with half the icing, then use the remaining
half to top the cake. Dust with cocoa powder for
a real cappuccino experience!

# SUNDAY CAKE

SERVES 8-10

Prep time: 15 minutes
Cooking time: 18–20 minutes

*You will need 2 × 21cm round loose-bottomed cake tins*

Ingredients:
170g unsalted butter, softened
170g caster sugar
3 eggs
140g self-raising flour, sifted
30g cocoa powder
1½ teaspoons baking powder

For the butter icing:
90g butter, softened
170g icing sugar
cocoa powder, to taste

For the topping:
200g milk chocolate

To decorate:
Buttons, Maltesers or Smarties

This is a cake that my mum made for us every Sunday growing up and for birthdays and special occasions. She would always make it in the morning, ready for our family who would come over to our house every Sunday, and she'd mix up the decorations for extra fun.

Preheat the oven to 180°C/350°F/GM4. Line the cake tins with greaseproof paper.

In a bowl cream together the butter and sugar until light and fluffy.

Add the eggs, sifted flour, cocoa powder and baking powder and mix until well combined.

Divide the batter between the two tins and spread with a spatula – don't worry if it doesn't reach the edges of the tin or seems very shallow, it will spread and rise in the oven. Bake for 18–20 minutes. Cool a little in the tin then transfer to a wire rack to cool completely.

For the butter icing, mix all the ingredients together until smooth.

Once the cake is completely cool, spread the icing over one cake and sandwich with the other.

For the topping, melt the chocolate in a bowl set over simmering water and pour it gently over the cake. Decorate with your favourite sweets.

# EARL GREY TEA LOAF

## SERVES 8-10

Prep time: 10 minutes
Cooking time: 40–50 minutes

*You will need a 22cm loaf tin*

50g butter, softened
100g light brown soft sugar
1 egg, beaten
zest and juice of 1 orange
300g mixed fruit
200ml strong Earl Grey tea
   left to stew overnight,
   then poured over the fruit
250g self-raising flour

When working on this book, I had a long lunch with my mum to discuss what recipes I should include. She said that when I was really small she'd always make her Earl Grey tea loaf and I would help in any way that I could. I so wish I could remember this, but it's before my earliest memory, though I love hearing Mum tell me stories about it. So I dedicate this recipe to my mum, and the times we baked this together.

Preheat the oven to 170°C/325°F/GM3. Line the loaf tin with greaseproof paper.

Cream together the butter and sugar in a bowl until light and fluffy. Mix in the egg, orange zest and juice and Earl Grey fruit mix, then fold in the flour until smooth.

Transfer to the tin and bake for 40–50 minutes, or until golden and risen and a skewer poked into the centre of the loaf comes out clean.

Allow to cool in the tin, then transfer to a wire rack to cool completely. Serve in slices spread with butter and a cup of tea.

# CHOCOLATE LOAF

SERVES 8-10

Prep time: 20 minutes
Cooking time: 50 minutes

. . . . . . . . . . . . .

*You will need a 22cm loaf tin*

Ingredients:
250g unsalted butter,
    softened, plus extra
    for greasing
100g white chocolate
100g milk chocolate
100g caramel-filled
    chocolate
200g caster sugar
4 eggs
1½ teaspoons baking powder
150g self-raising flour
60g cocoa powder

To decorate:
50g white chocolate

This is essentially my triple chocolate cookies in cake form. I love my cookies so much that one day I wondered what they'd be like in a dense, rich chocolate loaf cake. As you can imagine, it's chocolate heaven. I tried this out on my friend Emma after testing and she loved it!

. . . . . . . . . . . . .

Preheat the oven to 180°C/350°F/GM4. Lightly grease the loaf tin and line with greaseproof paper.

Using a knife, chop the white, milk and caramel chocolate into small chunks.

In a bowl, cream the butter and sugar until light and fluffy. Add the eggs, then fold in the baking powder, flour and cocoa until you have a smooth batter. Mix in the chocolate chunks until well dispersed. Pour into the tin and bake for 40–50 minutes, until risen and springy and a skewer poked into the centre of the loaf comes out clean.

Allow to cool in the tin, then transfer to a wire rack to cool completely.

To decorate, melt the white chocolate in a bowl set over a pan of simmering water, making sure the bottom of the bowl is not touching the water. Once melted, drizzle over the cooled loaf.

# LEMON DRIZZLE LOAF

### SERVES 8-10

Prep time: 15 minutes
Cooking time: 30 minutes

*You will need a 22cm loaf tin*

Ingredients:
170g unsalted butter,
   softened, plus extra
   for greasing
170g caster sugar
3 eggs
170g self-raising flour
1 teaspoon baking powder
zest of 2 lemons

For the drizzle:
150g icing sugar, plus
   extra for dusting
juice of 2 lemons

We've baked this for years in my family, as my dad is the biggest lemon fan. He always used to suck the fresh lemons and I was so impressed he could keep a straight face, as I could never do it. This loaf is perfect for all year round and is a lovely mix of moistness and crunchiness at the same time.

Preheat oven to 180°C/350°F/GM4. Lightly grease the loaf tin and line with greaseproof paper.

Cream together the butter and sugar, then mix in the eggs. Add the flour, baking powder and lemon zest and mix until smooth and well combined.

Pour the mixture into the tin and bake for 30 minutes, or until golden and risen and a skewer poked into the centre of the loaf comes out clean.

Mix together the icing sugar and lemon juice until smooth and the sugar has dissolved. While the loaf is still warm, poke holes into it with a skewer and pour over the drizzle.

Leave to cool in the tin, then turn out onto a plate and serve, dusted with icing sugar.

# PISTACHIO CAKE WITH LEMON CURD

SERVES 8-10

Prep time: 20 minutes
Cooking time: 40 minutes

*You will need a 21cm round
loose-bottomed cake tin*

Ingredients:
150g pistachios
200g unsalted butter,
    softened
200g caster sugar
2 large eggs
200g self-raising flour
zest of 1 lemon
1 jar of lemon curd

Fresh and zingy, with a wonderfully appetising colour, this is a really nice cake to try if you fancy something different. It works well served with a dollop of Greek yoghurt.

Preheat the oven to 180°C/350°F/GM4. Line the cake tin with greaseproof paper.

Put 100g of the pistachios into a food processor and whizz until finely ground (if you don't have a food processor, finely chop them instead). Set aside.

Cream together the butter and sugar until light and fluffy. Mix in the eggs, then add the flour, lemon zest and ground pistachios until well combined.

Pour into the prepared cake tin, smooth out as best you can and bake in the oven for 40 minutes until golden and springy and a skewer poked into the centre of the cake comes out clean.

Meanwhile, toast and chop the remaining 50g of pistachios.

Once the cake is out of the oven, immediately spread three-quarters of the jar of lemon curd over it and sprinkle over the chopped pistachios. Leave to cool completely in the tin, then turn out and serve each slice with a spoonful of the remaining lemon curd.

# MOCHA CAKE

SERVES 8-10

Prep time: 30 minutes
Cooking time: 25 minutes

*You will need 2 × 21cm round loose-bottomed cake tins*

Ingredients:
225g butter, softened
225g caster sugar
4 eggs
250g self-raising flour
50g cocoa powder
2 teaspoons baking powder
150ml strong coffee, cooled

For the icing:
250g butter, softened
440g icing sugar
60g cocoa powder

To decorate:
squirty cream and
   coffee beans

Funnily enough, although I love the flavour of coffee I am always the one ordering a decaf latté because caffeine doesn't agree with me. Every now and then, I'll switch my regular coffee order to a decaf mocha – so of course I had to represent this in cake form.

Preheat the oven to 180°C/350°F/GM4. Grease and line the cake tins.

Cream together the butter and sugar until light and fluffy. Mix in the eggs, then add the flour, cocoa powder and baking powder and combine. Slowly pour in the coffee and mix until you have a smooth batter.

Divide between the two cake tins and bake for 20–25 minutes until a skewer poked into the centre of the cake comes out clean. Cool in the tin then transfer to a wire rack to cool completely.

For the icing, in a bowl cream the butter and slowly add the icing sugar and cocoa powder until fully incorporated. Mix until light and smooth, then sandwich the two cakes together with half the icing. Use the remaining icing to top the cake and decorate with squirty cream and coffee beans, or whatever you fancy.

# CHERRY BUNDT CAKE

### SERVES 8-10

Prep time: 20 minutes
Cooking time: 35–40 minutes

*You will need a 23cm bundt tin*

Ingredients:
200g butter, softened,
    plus extra for greasing
250g glacé cherries
200g caster sugar
3 large eggs
250g self-raising flour
1 teaspoon baking powder
1 teaspoon vanilla extract
splash of full-fat milk

For the drizzle:
80g icing sugar

To decorate:
fresh or glacé cherries

For Christmas a couple of years ago, Jim's mum bought me a bundt cake tin. I'd never baked a bundt cake before, so was really excited to try one out. Of course there are so many different bundt cake recipes, but I love the traditional cherry; it looks so pretty, particularly when you cut into a slice.

Preheat the oven to 180°C/350°F/GM4. Grease the bundt tin and set aside.

Cut the cherries in half.

Cream together the butter and sugar until light and fluffy. Mix in the eggs, then add the flour, baking powder and vanilla extract and mix until well combined. Add a splash of milk and mix to form a smooth, wet batter.

Pour the mixture into a tin and bake for 35–40 minutes until a skewer poked into the centre of the cake comes out clean. Leave to cool in the tin.

Once cooled, make the drizzle. Mix a tablespoon of water into the icing sugar and mix thoroughly until you have a thick drizzle.

Turn the cake out onto a plate and drizzle the icing over the top. Decorate with fresh or glacé cherries and enjoy!

# FLOURLESS COCONUT & LIME CAKE

SERVES 8-10

Prep time: 20 minutes
Cooking time: 35–40 minutes

. . . . . . . . . . . . .

*You will need a 21cm round deep loose-bottomed cake tin*

Ingredients:
150g unsalted butter,
    softened, plus extra
    for greasing
4 eggs
150g golden caster sugar
150g ground almonds
100g dessicated coconut
zest and juice of 1 lime

For the topping:
200g icing sugar
zest and juice of 1 lime
a sprinkling of coconut flakes

This flavour combination makes me think of holidays, it's fresh, sweet and zingy all the same time - I think you guys are going to love it. Also, great news for those of you who are wheat intolerant, as this recipe is gluten free.

. . . . . . . . . . . . .

Preheat the oven to 180°C/350°F/GM4. Grease and line the cake tin with greaseproof paper.

Cream together the butter and eggs until light and fluffy. Add the sugar, ground almonds, desiccated coconut, lime juice and zest.

Pour into the cake tin and bake for 35–40 minutes until cooked through. Cool in the tin then transfer to a wire rack to cool completely.

For the topping, mix the icing sugar with the lime zest and juice – add a tiny bit of water if it's looking too thick. Pour this onto the cooled cake and sprinkle over the coconut flakes and any leftover zest to decorate.

# BROWNIE CAKE

SERVES 8-10

Prep time: 20 minutes
Cooking time: 30 minutes

*You will need a 21cm round
loose-bottomed cake tin*

Ingredients:
175g unsalted butter,
   plus extra for greasing
200g dark chocolate
   (70% cocoa solids)
200g light muscovado sugar
3 eggs
70g plain flour
1 tablespoon cocoa powder,
   plus extra for dusting
1 teaspoon baking powder
100g milk chocolate chips

To decorate:
cocoa powder or icing sugar

I'll never forget the night I went out to dinner at a cosy candlelit pub in Notting Hill and ate the most incredible brownie cake of my life. It was served warm with clotted cream and dusted with icing sugar and I knew right away that I was going to have to try to recreate it at home. I think it looks quite sophisticated to serve a brownie sliced if you are making it for dinner. I've made this for friends a few times and although it's quite rich, they always go for a second slice!

Preheat the oven to 160°C/325°F/GM3. Grease the cake tin with butter.

Break the chocolate into chunks and place in a medium pan. Add the butter and sugar and melt over a low heat, stirring, until fully combined. Remove from the heat.

Whisk the eggs, then mix into the chocolate mixture.

Stir in the flour, cocoa powder and baking powder, then fold in the chocolate chips.

Pour into the cake tin and bake for 30 minutes until a skewer poked into the centre of the cake comes out clean. Cool in the tin then transfer to a wire rack to cool completely, then dust generously with cocoa powder or icing sugar before cutting into slices.

# CARROT CAKE

SERVES 10-12

Prep time: 25 minutes
Cooking time: 20 minutes

*You will need 3 × 21cm round loose-bottomed cake tins*

Ingredients:
325g light muscovado sugar
25g plain flour
1½ teaspoons ground
    cinnamon
1 teaspoon ground ginger
1 teaspoon bicarbonate
    of soda
2 teaspoons baking powder
juice of 1 orange
3 large eggs
2 teaspoons vanilla extract
300ml vegetable oil
300g grated carrot
100g sultanas or raisins

For the icing:
125g butter, softened
300g icing sugar
150g full-fat cream cheese
1 teaspoon vanilla extract

To decorate:
chopped walnuts and pecans

Carrot cake always reminds me of when I worked at Jarrolds department store in Norwich, as I would often meet friends at the café next door, No. 33, on my break and we'd share a piece of one of their huge carrot cakes. They used to do the biggest slices and my favourite thing about it was the plump, juicy raisins inside, so I made sure when creating my own carrot cake recipe that I put them in.

Preheat the oven to 180°C/350°F/GM4. Line the cake tins with greaseproof paper.

In a bowl, combine the sugar, flour, spices, bicarbonate of soda and baking powder.

Add the orange juice, eggs and vanilla extract and mix through, then slowly add the oil, mixing as you go to form a smooth batter.

Fold through the carrot and sultanas or raisins. Divide the batter between the cake tins and spread until even. Bake for 18–20 minutes. Cool in the tin then transfer to a wire rack to cool completely.

For the icing, in a bowl cream together the butter and icing sugar until smooth and light. Add the cream cheese and vanilla extract and mix until smooth.

Sandwich the cakes together with the icing and add a final layer of icing on top. Decorate the top with pecans, walnuts and lemon zest, or even sprinkles if you have them.

# RAINBOW CAKE

SERVES 10-12

Prep time: 40 minutes
(if baking all at once)
Cooking time: 20 minutes

*You will need 7 × 21cm round loose-bottomed cake tins*

Ingredients (for 7 sponges):
675g butter, softened
675g caster sugar
12 eggs
3 teaspoons vanilla extract
675g self-raising flour
3 teaspoons baking powder
7 food colourings

For the icing:
600g unsalted butter,
    softened
1kg icing sugar
4 teaspoons vanilla extract

To decorate:
sprinkles

I wanted to dedicate a recipe to all of you who watch my videos, read my blog and interact with me on my social media accounts every day. I thought the perfect thing to make, just for you guys, would be rainbow cake, as so many of you sent me pictures of them when I first announced I was writing a baking book. A giant rainbow cake looks so bright and happy when you cut into it and that's how all of you make me feel every day!

Preheat the oven to 180°C/350°F/GM4. Grease and line the seven cake tins – if you don't have enough, you will have to make the cakes in batches.

In a large bowl, cream together the butter and sugar until light and fluffy, mix in the eggs and vanilla extract and finally add the flour and baking powder to form a smooth batter.

Divide the mixture equally between seven bowls. Add a few drops of food colouring to each bowl until you have the 7 different shades you're after.

Transfer the mixture to the cake tins, and bake in the oven for 180–20 minutes. Transfer the cakes to a wire rack and allow to cool.

To make the icing, cream the butter in a bowl and slowly add the icing sugar and vanilla extract. Beat until smooth and light – you may want to do this in batches as there's so much!

Use half the icing to sandwich the cakes together, then use the rest to ice the cake around the sides and on the top, smoothing it as you go. Decorate the top with sprinkles, if you like.

# AUSTRALIAN TOASTED BANANA BREAD

### SERVES 8-10

Prep time: 15 minutes
Cooking time: 40–50 minutes

. . . . . . . . . . . .

*You will need a 22cm loaf tin*

Ingredients:
350g peeled ripe bananas
150g butter, softened
160g dark brown soft sugar
2 large eggs
1 teaspoon vanilla extract
200g plain flour
2½ teaspoons baking powder
1 teaspoon salt
salted butter, to serve

In 2010, Jim and I spent six weeks in Sydney, Australia. We had the best time exploring the city and its beautiful beaches. It became a morning tradition to go down to the beach for coffee and banana bread and we'd try out all the different cafés. We decided our favourite was Gertrude and Alice, a quirky bookshop café with worn vintage sofas and cosy communal tables. On our return from Sydney, we were sort of in denial about being back, so we always used to bake banana bread to remind us of happy times at the beach. The Australians always toasted it and had it warm with melting butter on top and now this is the only way we eat it.

. . . . . . . . . . . .

Preheat the oven to 170°C/325°F/GM3. Grease and line the loaf tin with greaseproof paper.

Mash the bananas and set aside.

Cream together the butter and sugar until light and fluffy. Mix in the eggs and vanilla, then add the flour, baking powder and salt until combined.

Stir through the banana, then pour into the tin. Bake for 40–50 minutes, until risen and golden brown and a skewer poked into the centre of the loaf comes out clean.

Allow to cool completely, then toast the slices under a grill, spread with salted butter and enjoy!

# PLUM &
# ALMOND
# CAKE

SERVES 8-10

Prep time: 20 minutes
Cooking time: 40 minutes

*You will need a 21cm
round loose-bottomed cake tin*

Ingredients:
100g butter, softened
100g caster sugar
2 large eggs
2 tablespoons olive oil
75g plain flour
1 teaspoon baking powder
100g ground almonds, plus
    a sprinkling to decorate
5 plums, halved and destoned
4 tablespoons plum jam

To decorate:
flaked almonds
icing sugar

I was inspired to make a plum cake after trying my friend Emma's plum cake creation in Walberswick. Emma hates baking, as she doesn't like to measure anything, however this cake turned out to be the tastiest surprise. As you can imagine, she couldn't tell me her recipe as she didn't know it herself! So this is my version with some added almonds.

Preheat oven to 180°C/350°F/GM4. Line the cake tin with greaseproof paper.

In a bowl, cream together the butter and sugar until light and fluffy, then fold in the eggs and oil.

Add the flour, baking powder and ground almonds and combine well.

Spoon the mixture into the tin and spread out evenly with a spatula. Sprinkle over some additional ground almonds, then place the plums on top, round side up (you don't need to press them into the cake mixture). Bake for 35–40 minutes.

Warm up the plum jam in the microwave for 30 seconds, then brush over the cake with a pastry brush. Scatter with flaked almonds, and leave to cool completely in the tin.

Dust with icing sugar when ready to serve.

# GINGERBREAD LOAF

SERVES 6-8

Prep time: 15 minutes
Cooking time: 30 minutes.

. . . . . . . . . . . . .

*You will need a 22cm loaf tin*

Ingredients:
100g butter
100g golden syrup
150g self-raising flour
3 teaspoons ground ginger
150g caster sugar
1 teaspoon bicarbonate
   of soda
150ml milk
1 large egg

My grandad is obsessed with his breadmaker, freshly baked loaves are delivered to my parents' house almost daily. One time he experimented with his breadmaker and made a gingerbread loaf, it was so moist, sticky and delicious that I requested he make it all the time. Now whenever I eat gingerbread, it makes me think of my grandad. I hope he thinks my recipe is as good as his breadmaker one.

. . . . . . . . . . . . .

Preheat the oven to 180°C/350°F/GM4. Line the loaf tin with greaseproof paper.

Melt the butter and golden syrup together in a pan and set aside.

Mix together the flour, ground ginger, sugar and bicarbonate of soda in a bowl, then slowly whisk in the milk and egg, followed by the syrup mixture, to form a smooth batter.

Pour into the loaf tin and bake for 30–35 minutes, until golden and a skewer poked into the centre of the loaf comes out clean. Leave to cool completely.

# VICTORIA SPONGE CAKE

### SERVES 8-10

Prep time: 15 minutes
Cooking time: 25 minutes

*You will need 2 × 21cm round loose-bottomed cake tins*

Ingredients:
225g unsalted butter,
   softened
225g caster sugar
4 eggs
1 teaspoon vanilla extract
225g self-raising flour
1 teaspoon baking powder
pinch of salt

For the filling:
200ml double cream
1 jar strawberry jam
1 punnet fresh strawberries,
   hulled and halved

To decorate:
a couple of strawberries,
   hulled and halved
icing sugar, for dusting

If I am having friends for afternoon tea, this is the first cake that pops into my head to make. It's such a classic and so beautiful to look at, it will always be one of my favourites.

Preheat the oven to 180°C/350°F/GM4. Grease the cake tins and line with greaseproof paper.

Cream together the butter and sugar until light and fluffy. Whisk in the eggs and vanilla extract, then mix in the flour, baking powder and salt until you have a smooth batter.

Divide between the two tins and bake in the centre of the oven for 25 minutes, or until risen, springy and golden and a skewer poked into the centre of the cake comes out clean. Cool in the tin then transfer to a wire rack to cool completely.

For the filling, whisk the cream in a bowl until thick and peaks form. Spread one cake with a thick layer of strawberry jam, then gently lay the cream on top. Note that the cream and jam don't need to completely reach the edge of the sponge as both will spread once the cake is cut.

Add a layer of strawberries, and gently rest the other cake on top.

Pop a couple of strawberries on the top and dust with icing sugar to serve.

# SUPER DUPER CHOCOLATE CAKE

SERVES 10-12

Prep time: 40 minutes
Cooking time: 18–20 minutes

*You will need 3 × 21cm round loose-bottomed cake tins*

Ingredients:
200ml full-fat milk
100g dark chocolate
 (70% cocoa solids)
300g plain flour
75g cocoa powder
3 teaspoons baking powder
1½ teaspoons bicarbonate
 of soda
375g caster sugar
200ml vegetable oil
3 large eggs
200g Greek yoghurt
2 teaspoons vanilla extract

For the icing:
200g white chocolate
250g salted butter, softened
600g sifted icing sugar

To decorate:
chocolate shavings

I feel so excited about this recipe, I had such a strong vision for what I wanted. I envisaged the cake being really dark chocolate with white chocolate icing so that when you cut into it you see magnificient contrasting layers. When it came to making the cake, it was the aesthetic that made it come to life in my head, so when I'd finish making it and it was time for the taste test I was over the moon that it turned out to be wow, wow and wow again! It's really hard to describe quite how delicious this cake is, you'll just have to make it and find out for yourselves.

Preheat the oven to 180°C/350°F/GM4. Line the cake tins with greaseproof paper.

Put the milk in a pan and bring to simmering point. Take off the heat, add the dark chocolate and leave to melt. Mix until well combined and smooth.

Mix the flour, cocoa powder, baking powder and bicarbonate of soda in a bowl.

In a separate bowl, whisk the oil, eggs, yoghurt and vanilla extract. Slowly add the chocolate mixture until well combined, then fold in the flour, cocoa powder, baking powder and bicarbonate of soda and mix to a smooth batter.

Divide evenly between the cake tins and bake for 18–20 minutes. Transfer the cakes to a wire rack to cool.

To make the icing, first melt the white chocolate in a bowl set over a pan of simmering water, making sure the bottom of the bowl isn't touching the water. In another bowl, whisk the butter and icing sugar well until smooth and light, then add the melted chocolate and stir until well combined. Layer the cakes together with the icing and spread some on the top then decorate with chocolate shavings.

# PUDDINGS

# "A spoonful of sugar"

JIM'S MUM'S BANOFFEE PIE

SALTED CARAMEL CHEESECAKE

BAILEYS TIRAMISU

LEMON MERINGUE PIE

STICKY TOFFEE PUDDING

PINEAPPLE UPSIDE-DOWN CAKE

MARMALADE BREAD & BUTTER PUDDING

AUTUMN PAVLOVA

MADDIE'S MUM'S CHOCOLATE ROULADE

CHOCOLATE ORANGE CHEESECAKE

APPLE & BLACKBERRY CRUMBLE

NIGELLA'S COOKIE DOUGH POTS

# JIM'S MUM'S BANOFFEE PIE

### SERVES: 8–10

Prep time: 20 minutes
Chilling time: 45 minutes

*You will need a 21cm round loose-bottomed tart tin*

Ingredients:
400g chocolate Hobnobs
150g butter
1 tin (397g) Carnation caramel
4 ripe bananas
400ml double cream
1 chocolate flake

I remember the first time Jim's mum Judy placed her famous banoffee pie on the table. She cut me an enormous slice and I devoured every mouthful. The next time we had it, Jim and I asked if we could make it with her instructions and it turns out it was one of the easiest things I've ever made. It's simply a case of assembling the ingredients, but my goodness will it blow your mind!

Crumble the Hobnobs into a bowl. Melt the butter and mix with the Hobnobs until well dispersed, then press into the bottom of the tart tin and bring up the sides to help keep the filling secure. Transfer to the fridge to chill and set for 30 minutes.

Pour the jar of Carnation caramel on top of the base and spread it out evenly. Pop in the fridge for 15 minutes to set the caramel slightly.

When ready to serve, slice the bananas thinly then layer them on top of the caramel.

Whip the cream in a bowl until soft peaks form, then dollop on top of the banana.

Break up the flake over the top and serve immediately.

# SALTED CARAMEL CHEESECAKE

## SERVES 10-12

Prep time: 25 minutes
Cooking time: 40 minutes
Chilling time: at least 4 hours

*You will need a 21cm round loose-bottomed cake tin*

Ingredients:
260g chocolate Hobnobs
  (1 pack)
100g butter, melted
600g cream cheese
250g caster sugar
3 large eggs
150g Carnation caramel
1 teaspoon vanilla extract
1 teaspoon sea salt flakes,
  plus a little more to serve

For the glaze:
250g Carnation caramel
3 tablespoons double cream

This recipe is inspired by The Cheesecake Factory in LA. It's such a fun restaurant with a fridge packed full of the most decadent cheesecakes. When I stay in West Hollywood, sometimes I'll pop down to The Grove and get a slice to take away. When deciding what flavour to make my baked cheesecake for this book, I quickly settled on salted caramel. I'm a bit of a salted caramel addict, as I am sure a lot of you are! I decided to make this with a chocolate Hobnob base rather than just plain old digestives, to add a little extra something.

Preheat the oven to 180°C/350°F/GM4.

Crumble the Hobnobs in a bowl. Add the melted butter and press the base mixture evenly into the bottom of the cake tin. Bake for 10 minutes.

In a bowl, blend together the cream cheese and sugar, then add the eggs. Mix in the caramel, vanilla and salt until well combined, then spread evenly over the biscuit base.

Bake for 40 minutes until risen and browned on top. Leave to cool in the oven completely – this will help to prevent cracks appearing as the cake cools.

For the caramel glaze, heat up the caramel and cream together in a pan and stir to blend. Pour the glaze over the cooled cheesecake, then refrigerate for at least 4 hours or preferably overnight. Sprinkle with extra sea salt flakes when you're ready to serve.

# BAILEYS TIRAMISU

SERVES 8-10

Prep time: 20 minutes
Chilling time: at least 2 hours

. . . . . . . . . . . . .

*You will need a 21 × 21 × 5cm glass dish*

Ingredients:
300ml strong coffee
200ml Baileys
250ml double cream
250g mascarpone cheese
75g golden caster sugar
400g chocolate sponge fingers
cocoa powder, to dust

On New Year's Eve I entered a pudding competition with my friends Kate and Scarlett and I am very proud to say, we won! Our tiramisu was epic and was the first pudding to be completely demolished. It was so fun to make. I was on slicing cake duty, Kate was on dipping duty and Scarlett was on whipping duty – then we all helped to assemble our creation together. I had the idea to change the traditional Tia Maria ingredient to Baileys as it's one of my favourite alcoholic drinks and it works brilliantly. My friend Maddie gave me the idea to use chocolate sponge instead of the traditional lady's fingers, which makes the tiramisu taste even more indulgent. Maddie swears by the McVities chocolate loaf cake. You'll be pleased to know there's no need to make your own sponge for this as shop-bought actually works better, it's more absorbent and doesn't fall apart in the dipping process.

. . . . . . . . . . . . .

Mix the coffee with 140ml of the Baileys in a shallow bowl and set aside.

Whip the double cream until it forms soft peaks, then add the mascarpone, caster sugar and remaining Baileys and beat again until thick.

Now, start layering. Dip the sponge fingers one at a time into the coffee mix, and use them to line the bottom of your serving dish. Spoon in half the cream mixture and spread out until even. Repeat the process, this time with a double layer of sponge fingers. Top with the remaining cream and refrigerate for 2 hours or until needed (this can be chilled overnight).

Just before serving, dust with cocoa powder.

# LEMON MERINGUE PIE

SERVES 6-8

Prep time: 30 minutes
Chilling time: at least
30 minutes
Cooking time: 20 minutes

*You will need a 30cm round
pie dish or loose-bottomed
tart tin*

Ingredients:
400g digestive biscuits
200g butter, melted
2 tablespoons cornflour
zest and juice of 3 large
    lemons
120g golden caster sugar
100g butter
1 egg, plus 3 egg yolks
    and 4 egg whites
200g caster sugar

When I told my dad I was writing a baking book, he said only three words to me. Lemon meringue pie. Then he quickly added, with a biscuit bottom! As I have mentioned elsewhere, my dad is the biggest lemon lover and his ultimate lemon dessert is lemon meringue pie. It's traditionally made with a pastry base, however, he tried it once with a biscuit bottom and said it was a game changer, so requested I made one with biscuit for my book.

Crumb the biscuits and mix in the melted butter until well combined. Press into the base and sides of a pie dish, then chill in the fridge for at least 30 minutes.

Preheat the oven to 180°C/350°F/GM4.

To make the filling, mix the cornflour, lemon zest and juice, golden caster sugar and 200ml of water in a pan over a medium flame until smooth and thickened.

Take off the heat and stir in the butter until melted. Whisk together the egg yolks and whole egg and stir into the lemon mix. Put back on the heat and cook for a few minutes, stirring constantly, until thickened to a consistency similar to custard.

Leave to cool for a minute, then pour into the chilled pie base. Set aside.

To make the meringue, in a clean dry bowl, whisk the egg whites to soft peaks then add the sugar, a tablespoon at a time, and whisk until glossy and thick. Spoon onto the tart, spread it carefully and give it a few decorative swirls.

Bake in the middle of the oven for 20 minutes until the meringue is golden, then leave to cool completely before serving in the dish or remove it from the tin.

# STICKY TOFFEE PUDDING

MAKES 6

This is Jim's number one pudding. His favourite sticky toffee pudding is served at a restaurant called Hawksmoor in London. I have to agree with him, it is fantastic, so the bar was set very high for me to try to come up with something that was just as good. This pudding took quite a few attempts to get right but I'm happy to say we're finally there. It's warm, sticky, oozy and like a hug in a bowl. Jim likes his served with vanilla ice-cream.

Prep time: 15 minutes
Cooking time: 20 minutes

*You will need 6 × 7cm ovenproof ramekins*

Ingredients:
75g salted butter, softened
150g dark muscovado sugar
2 eggs
150ml full-fat milk
1 teaspoon vanilla extract
200g self-raising flour

For the sauce:
80g butter
100g dark brown
   muscovado sugar
2 tablespoons golden syrup
150ml double cream

vanilla ice-cream, to serve

Preheat the oven to 180°C/350°F/GM4. Grease six ramekins.

In a bowl, cream together the butter and sugar until light and fluffy. Mix in the eggs, milk and vanilla until combined, then fold in the flour to form a smooth batter.

Divide between the six ramekins, place on a baking tray and bake for 20 minutes until risen and golden.

While the puddings are in the oven, make the sauce. Melt the butter, sugar and golden syrup in a pan over a low heat until melted and smooth, then mix in the cream. Keep warm until the puddings are ready.

Serve the puddings immediately by turning them out onto individual serving plates and coating them in the sauce. Serve with vanilla ice-cream.

# PINEAPPLE UPSIDE-DOWN CAKE

### SERVES 6-8

Prep time: 25 minutes
Cooking time: 30–35 minutes

. . . . . . . . . . . . . .

*You will need a 21cm
round loose-bottomed cake tin*

Ingredients:
150g soft butter, plus
    extra for greasing
3 tablespoons golden syrup
6 slices tinned pineapple
    (reserve the juice)
6 glacé cherries
150g golden caster sugar
2 eggs
150g plain flour
1½ teaspoons baking powder
60ml pineapple juice
splash of spiced rum (optional)

crème fraîche, to serve

At our primary school, we had the choice between hot dinners or packed lunch. I usually opted for hot dinners and our arts and crafts helper Mrs Austen created a really cool system for how we selected what we wanted. She made a cardboard wall display with multi-coloured pockets for all the options, and you put your tickets (one for main, one for dessert) in the pockets to show what you wanted. There were usually two dessert options, either a bowl of fruit (boring!) or some kind of delicious pudding. There were two puddings that would make me jump up and down if I saw them on the label, obviously one being chocolate pudding and chocolate sauce (every kids' favourite) and every now and then, Pineapple Upside Down Cake. This was our school chef, Mrs Roberts' speciality. Sweet, baked, syrupy pineapple on top of the softest, warm vanilla sponge cake with rivers of hot custard. When I make it at home, it reminds me of those happy school days.

. . . . . . . . . . . . .

Preheat the oven to 200°C/400°F/GM6. Grease the cake tin well. Microwave the golden syrup for 20 seconds, or heat it gently in a pan. Pour into the cake tin and tilt around to cover the bottom.

Pat the pineapple rings dry with kitchen paper and arrange on the bottom of the tin. Pop a cherry into the centre of each ring and drizzle a little rum over the pineapple rings, if using.

In a bowl, cream together the butter and sugar until light and fluffy. Beat in the eggs, then add the flour and baking powder. Slowly pour in the pineapple juice and beat to form a smooth dough.

Pour into the cake tin, smooth over and bake for 30–35 minutes until the cake is risen and golden.

Use a spatula to loosen the edges of the cake, then turn out onto a plate so that the pineapple rings are on top. Serve with crème fraîche.

# MARMALADE BREAD & BUTTER PUDDING

### SERVES 6-8

Prep time: 20 minutes
Cooking time: 35 minutes

. . . . . . . . . . . . .

*You will need a 30cm pie dish*

Ingredients:
50g butter, melted, plus
    extra for greasing
10 slices white bread
1 teaspoon ground cinnamon
1 teaspoon ground nutmeg
300ml full-fat milk
100ml double cream
2 eggs
100g golden caster sugar
4 tablespoons marmalade

custard, cream or ice-cream,
    to serve

Last year, Jim and I spent a glorious 24 hours staying in a log cabin in the countryside at Soho Farm House. After a day of spa treatments and hanging out with the farm horses, we headed to the barn for dinner. We sat in front of a crackling fire and had one of the most gorgeous three-course meals we had ever eaten. We shared their marmalade bread and butter pudding and were blown away. I didn't think it would be too hard to try to recreate this at home, especially as I already had an old family bread and butter pudding recipe. So I added the marmalade to it and it turned out to be one of the tastiest puddings I've ever made. Bread and butter pudding to me is real comfort food and I am so happy that I discovered the marmalade version, as it really takes it to another level.

. . . . . . . . . . . . .

Grease the pie dish.

Remove the crusts from the bread and cut each piece into four triangles.

Put a layer of bread in the bottom of the dish, then brush with melted butter. Sprinkle over some cinnamon and nutmeg, then repeat the process. Keep going until you have three layers of bread.

In a pan, warm the milk and cream together, but don't let it boil.

Whisk the eggs and sugar together until light and pale, then slowly pour this into the cream mixture, stirring constantly, until fully combined.

Pour the custard over the bread slices. At this point, turn on the oven to 180°C/350°F/GM4. Allow the bread pudding to sit while the oven heats up.

Bake for 25–30 minutes until the top is golden brown. Warm up the marmalade , then brush over the top of the pudding. Return to the oven for 5 minutes more.

Serve with custard, cream, ice-cream, or all three!

# AUTUMN PAVLOVA

SERVES 8-10

Pavlova is a dessert normally associated with summer. One autumn day when I was having the girls over for a dinner party, I was coming up with my menu and with English blackberries and pears in season, I decided pavlova would be a great option. With lemon curd to cut through the sweetness and added hazelnuts for a bit of crunch and texture, this is an amazing dessert. When I placed this dish on the table the girls named it Octopud as the way I had arranged the pears made it look like an octopus!

Prep time: 40 minutes
Cooking time: 1 hour

Ingredients:
6 large egg whites
300g caster sugar

For the topping:
2 Earl Grey tea bags
100g caster sugar
2 Conference pears, peeled
   with stem left on
500ml double cream
300g lemon curd
150g blackberries
15g toasted hazelnuts

Preheat the oven to 150°C/300°F/GM2. Line a large baking tray with greaseproof paper.

In a clean dry bowl, whisk the egg whites until stiff peaks form, then add the caster sugar, a tablespoon at a time, and whisk until smooth and glossy.

Spoon the meringue onto the baking tray and swirl it into a circle, making a dent in the middle. Shape the edge of the meringue into swirls using a spatula, then place on the middle shelf in the oven and bake for 1 hour. Let the meringue cool completely in the oven without opening the oven door.

Meanwhile, prepare the topping. Boil 500ml water, add the tea bags, remove from the heat and steep for 10 minutes. Discard the tea bags, add the sugar and pears to the tea, then return to a low heat and gently simmer for 20 minutes until the pear is tender. Remove the pears and set aside to cool, then chop into chunks. Put the syrup over a high heat and boil for 20 minutes until reduced and sticky.

Once the meringue is completely cool, whip the cream until it forms soft peaks. Spoon onto the meringue, then top with most of the lemon curd, reserving a few tablespoons. Swirl the cream and lemon curd mixture across the meringue, then top with the chopped pear, blackberries and hazelnuts.

Finish by drizzling over the reserved lemon curd and a few tablespoons of the Earl Grey syrup.

# MADDIE'S MUM'S CHOCOLATE ROULADE

SERVES 6-8

Prep time: 20 minutes
Cooking time: 20 minutes

. . . . . . . . . . . .

*You will need a Swiss roll tin*

Ingredients:
200g dark chocolate
    (70% cocoa solids)
4 large eggs
125g caster sugar
200ml double cream
cocoa powder, to dust

As teenagers, one of my best friends Maddie and I would be lucky enough to experience her mum's famous chocolate roulade at any birthday or other celebratory occasion. I have to say, we never helped her make it, we were probably too busy being grumpy teenagers, so in the process of writing this book, I had to call Vicky, Maddie's mum, and ask her for her recipe, along with the step-by-step guide of how to make it. I always remember it being so rich, chocolatey and moist. Vicky often decorated hers with Thorntons chocolates along the top.

. . . . . . . . . . . .

Preheat the oven to 180°C/350°F/GM4. Line a Swiss roll tin with greaseproof paper.

Break the chocolate into small pieces and melt in a bowl set over a pan of simmering water, making sure that the bottom of the bowl isn't touching the water. Once melted, set aside to cool slightly.

Separate the eggs into 2 large bowls. Whisk the egg yolks with the sugar for 2 minutes, until the mixture is pale and leaves a ribbon off your whisk.

Whisk the egg whites in a clean dry bowl until soft peaks form.

Add the melted chocolate to the egg yolks and sugar, stirring gently to combine. Fold in a large tablespoon of the egg whites, then fold in the rest with a metal spoon, taking care to knock out as little air as possible.

Pour the mixture into the Swiss roll tin and spread evenly. Bake for 20 minutes until firm, then leave to cool in the tin.

Whisk the double cream until thick. Turn out the cooled roulade onto a sheet of greaseproof paper and spread the cream evenly over the roulade. Roll up the roulade using the paper to help, and don't worry if the sponge cracks – this is typical of a roulade!

Transfer to a serving plate and dust with cocoa powder to serve.

# CHOCOLATE ORANGE CHEESECAKE

### SERVES 8-10

Prep time: 20 minutes
Setting time: at least 2 hours

*You will need a 21cm round
loose-bottomed cake tin*

Ingredients:
300g double chocolate
　cookies
100g butter, melted
zest of 2 oranges
250g full-fat cream cheese
150g icing sugar
200g Terry's Chocolate
　Orange, plus extra 'slices'
　for decorating
150g double cream

Although you can get them all year round,
I always used to get (and still do) a Terry's
Chocolate Orange in my stocking and I don't think
I would ever eat one at any other time of the year,
as I associate them with Christmas. However,
when incorporated into a cheesecake, I'm willing
to break the rules. The flavour of this cheesecake
is mouthwateringly good, it also needs no baking
and I really enjoy breaking up the segments and
decorating it. One for me, one for the cheesecake…

Crush the biscuits to crumbs. Mix in the melted
butter and zest of 1 orange until well combined,
then press into the bottom of the tin.

Mix together the cream cheese and icing sugar
until smooth. Set aside.

Melt the 200g of Chocolate Orange in a bowl
set over a pan of simmering water, making sure
the bottom of the bowl isn't touching the water.
Once melted, quickly whip the cream in a bowl
until it forms soft peaks, then add the melted
chocolate and cream cheese mixture. Mix until
smooth and well combined.

Pour onto the biscuit base and smooth out.
Chill in the fridge for at least 2 hours.

When you're ready to serve, decorate with
the remaining Chocolate Orange slices and
orange zest.

# APPLE & BLACKBERRY CRUMBLE

SERVES 8

Prep time: 15 minutes
Cooking time: 45 minutes

. . . . . . . . . . . . .

*You will need a 22cm square
ovenproof dish*

Ingredients:
4 Bramley apples,
 peel left on
1 punnet blackberries
½ teaspoon ground
 cinnamon
100g plain flour
1 teaspoon baking powder
100g cold butter
75g demerara sugar
50g granulated sugar

custard, cream or ice-cream,
 to serve

There's nothing more warming and comforting on a chilly winter's day than a fruit crumble and custard. I love the colour that the blackberries bring to this crumble and apple is my favourite flavour when it comes to warm fruit. This crumble topping is my Mum's recipe that I've always eaten growing up.

. . . . . . . . . . . . .

Preheat the oven to 170°C/325°F/GM3.

Core and chop your Bramley apples roughly and put them in the bottom of a baking dish along with the blackberries, then sprinkle over the cinnamon.

Place the flour, baking powder and butter in a food processor, and whizz to incorporate, or rub the butter into the flour and baking powder to crumbs. Stir through the sugar.

Spread the crumble over the fruit, then bake in the oven for 45 minutes, until the topping is crunchy and golden.

Serve with custard, cream or ice-cream – or all three!

# NIGELLA'S COOKIE DOUGH POTS

MAKES 6 POTS

Prep time: 15 minutes
Cooking time: 10 minutes

. . . . . . . . . . . . . .

*You will need 6 × 7cm ramekins*

Ingredients:
110g unsalted butter,
    softened, plus extra
    for greasing
85g soft light brown sugar
1 large egg
1 teaspoon vanilla extract
150g plain flour
½ teaspoon bicarbonate
    of soda
½ teaspoon sea salt
80g white chocolate chips
80g milk chocolate chips

cream or ice-cream,
    to serve

I wanted most of the recipes in this book to be ones I had created myself or ones that were passed on to me by family and friends. I think, however, this is one of the most ingenious recipes created by Nigella and I wanted to help spread the word about how good it is. Nigella says these cookie dough pots are the solution for making incredibly gooey cookies that wouldn't otherwise keep their shape if they were cooked loose on a tray. I changed one thing from Nigella's recipe, and that's the chocolate, she went for dark and I went for a combination of milk and white as that's what I fancied on the day I was making these. I love seeing the different colours of the melted chocolate as I dig my spoon into the pot.

. . . . . . . . . . . . . .

Preheat the oven to 180°C/350°F/GM4 and grease six ramekins.

In a bowl, cream together the butter and sugar until light and creamy, then mix in the egg and vanilla. Fold in the flour, bicarbonate of soda and salt, until well combined, then mix through the chocolate chips.

Divide the mixture between the ramekins and bake for 10 minutes, until the top is golden.

Serve immediately with cream or ice-cream.

# PASTRY

# "No soggy bottoms"

NANNY'S APPLE PIE

LEMON TART

STRAWBERRY TARTS

CUSTARD TARTS

TARTE TATIN

PUMPKIN PIE

PECAN PIE

PROFITEROLES

SALTED CHOCOLATE TART

# NANNY'S APPLE PIE

SERVES 8

Prep time: 40 minutes
Chilling time: 30 minutes
Cooking time: 20 minutes

*You will need a 25cm pie dish*

Ingredients:
340g plain flour, plus extra
  for dusting
110g cold vegetable fat
60g cold butter, plus extra
  for greasing
5 cooking apples
2 tablespoons
  granulated sugar
1 egg, beaten

ice-cream, cream or custard,
  to serve

Growing up my nanny always used to cook apple pie for us for Sunday lunch. Out of the whole family, I was the most crazy about this pie and always looked forward to it. When I was writing my first book, *Love, Tanya*, I went to her house and we baked her recipe together and Jim took a photo of us in the garden with her pie to include in the book. It really is incredible, I recommend it warm from the oven on a Sunday, with custard or vanilla ice-cream.

In a bowl, mix the flour, fat and butter with your fingers until crumbly. Add 6 tablespoons of water and mix together to make a ball of pastry. Wrap in clingfilm and chill in the fridge for 30 minutes.

Preheat the oven to 200°C/400°F/GM6.

Peel and chop the apples into bite-sized chunks and put in a pan with a tablespoon of water and the sugar. Cook over a high heat for 10 minutes until the apples are soft. Set aside to cool.

Take the pastry from the fridge, and divide into two pieces, one slightly bigger than the other.

Grease the pie dish and roll out the larger piece of pastry on a floured surface into a circle large enough to overhang the dish. Place in the dish so the pastry hangs over the edge. Fill with the apple and brush the edges with egg.

Roll out the smaller piece of pastry into a circle that sits easily on top, then crimp the sides to attach the top and bottom. Trim off the excess pastry. Pierce a hole in the top to let out the steam, and brush the pastry with egg. If you like, cut out a few leaves with the excess pastry to make a pretty design for the top. Secure with water and brush with egg as before.

Bake for 20 minutes, turning down the oven to 170°C/325°F/GM3 for the last 10 minutes until the pie is golden brown. Serve with ice-cream, cream or custard.

# LEMON TART

Prep time: 25 minutes
Chilling time: 30 minutes
Cooking time: 50 minutes

*You will need a 25cm round loose-bottomed tart tin and some baking beans*

Ingredients:
220g plain flour, plus
    extra for dusting
120g butter
30g caster sugar
1 egg
icing sugar, to dust

For the filling:
5 lemons, zest and juice
6 eggs
300g caster sugar
250ml double cream

The night before Jim and I got married, we had a barbecue in the Walled Garden at Babington House with all our closest friends and family. It was September and we were hoping for sun, however it was kind of chilly and drizzling with rain. This didn't stop us from having one of the most lovely and memorable evenings of our lives. The garden was covered in fairy lights and we all wrapped up in cosy blankets and sheltered under umbrellas. We had three desserts on the menu and lemon tart was one of them. This was my favourite, and I wanted to include a lemon tart recipe here to remind me of that special evening.

Put the flour, butter and sugar in a food processor and whizz until combined. Add the egg and 3 tablespoons of water and whizz again to form a dough.

Roll out the pastry on a floured surface to a thickness of about 3–4mm and put in the tart tin. Press gently into each crevice and leave the excess hanging over the edge. Chill in the fridge for 30 minutes.

Preheat the oven to 180°C/350°F/GM4, then line the pastry with greaseproof paper before filling with baking beans. Bake for 10 minutes before removing the beans, pricking the base with a fork and baking for another 10 minutes until the pastry is golden and completely dry.

Using a serrated knife, cut off the excess pastry to leave a neat edge. Set the tart case aside.

Turn down the oven to 160°C/325°F/GM3.

Put all the filling ingredients into a bowl and whisk until smooth.

Pour into the pastry case and tap the case gently to get rid of any air bubbles. Bake for 30 minutes, or until just set with a slight wobble.

Leave to cool completely, then remove from the tin and dust with icing sugar to serve.

# STRAWBERRY TARTS

MAKES 4

Prep time: 30 minutes
Chilling time: 30 minutes
Cooking time: 20 minutes

*You will need 4 individual 10cm loose-bottomed tartlet tins and some baking beans*

For the pastry:
340g plain flour, plus
    extra for dusting
100g cold vegetable fat
60g cold butter

For the filling:
good-quality thick custard
1 punnet strawberries
1 tablespoon seedless
    strawberry jam
icing sugar, to dust

These remind me of being in Paris and peering through French patisserie windows after a trip to my favourite museum, the Musée d'Orsay.

. . . . . . . . . . . . .

In a bowl, mix the flour, fat and butter together with your fingers until crumbly. Add 100ml cold water and mix again to form a pastry. Wrap in clingfilm and chill for 30 minutes.

Preheat the oven to 180°C/350°F/GM4.

Roll out the pastry thinly on a floured surface, and cut out 4 circles a little larger than the tartlet tins. Line the tins, leaving the excess pastry hanging over the edge. Gently press the pastry into the sides.

Line the pastry with greaseproof paper and fill with baking beans. Bake for 10 minutes before removing the beans, pricking the base with a fork and baking until golden brown. Cut off the excess pastry with a serrated knife to form a neat edge and set aside to cool completely.

Once cooled, spoon 2 tablespoons of custard into each case and smooth out.

Slice the strawberries thinly and arrange on top of the custard in your preferred pattern.

Heat the jam in the microwave for 30 seconds, or in a pan until runny, then brush over the strawberries.

Chill until needed. To serve, remove the tart tins and dust with icing sugar.

# CUSTARD TARTS

MAKES 12

Prep time: 25 minutes
Cooking time: 20 minutes

*You will need a 12-hole cupcake/muffin tray*

Ingredients:
250ml full-fat milk
pinch of ground cinnamon
seeds from 1 vanilla pod, or
    1 teaspoon vanilla purée
40g plain flour
3 egg yolks
butter, for greasing
1 sheet ready-rolled
    all-butter puff pastry
200g caster sugar
1 egg, for brushing

These little custard tarts are practically bite-sized and are so delicious with the creamy custard centre and crisp layers encasing it you might need more than one.

Warm the milk, cinnamon and vanilla gently in a pan until almost to the boil. Take off the heat.

Add the flour to a second pan, and add a splash of the hot milk. Mix to form a paste, then slowly add the remaining milk, stirring as you go until the mixture has thickened. Set aside.

Put the sugar and 100ml water in another pan and put over a low heat until the sugar has melted. Increase the heat and boil for 4–5 minutes until the sugar is syrupy - be careful as it's incredibly hot.

Slowly add the sugar mixture to the milk and mix well. Strain the mixture into a jug to get rid of any lumps.

Put the egg yolks in a large bowl and whisk. Slowly add the milk mixture until fully incorporated, then cover with clingfilm and chill for 30 minutes or until needed.

Preheat the oven to its highest setting and put a baking tray in to preheat, too. Grease the muffin tray.

Unroll the pastry, remove the paper inside, then roll the pastry back up as tightly as possible. Cut the roll in half, then cut each half into six so you have 12 slices altogether. Using your hands, flatten each slice as thinly as possible, then use them to line the holes of your muffin tray, pressing into each crevice.

Divide the custard mixture between each pastry case, leaving 1cm of the rim exposed. Brush the exposed pastry with a beaten egg as well as you can.

Bake for 20 minutes, placing the muffin tray on top of the preheated baking tray. The tarts are ready when they're golden and crispy.

# TARTE TATIN

Prep time: 20 minutes
Cooling time: 10 minutes
Cooking time: 30 minutes

*You will need an ovenproof frying pan*

Ingredients:
6 apples of different
    varieties if possible,
    sharp and sweet
50g butter
150g soft light brown sugar
1 vanilla pod
block of ready-made
    puff pastry
flour, for dusting
½ teaspoon ground
    cinnamon

vanilla ice-cream, to serve

This was one of the last recipes to make it into this book. On one of the baking photoshoots, I asked the team at Penguin publishers if they felt anything was missing from the book and the photographer, Susanna, food stylist Charlie and art director Emma all cried Tarte Tatin! They said it was their all-time favourite dessert to order at a restaurant but not something they'd ever make at home. I decided to give it a go and it turned out to be easy and delicious.

Preheat the oven to 200°C/400°F/GM6.

Peel your apples, core them, then cut them in half.

Place the butter and sugar in the frying pan along with 50ml water. Cut the vanilla pod in half lengthways, scrape out the seeds and add to the pan. Put over a medium heat and stir until golden and syrupy, then add the apples – you might like to cut a few into smaller pieces to fill any gaps. Coat the apples in the caramel and fry for 5 minutes until the apples are starting to soften. Take off the heat and leave to cool completely.

Roll out the pastry on a floured surface to ½cm thick and cut out a circle big enough to cover your frying pan, with some extra draping over. Place the pastry on top of the pan and tuck in the edges around the fruit. Bake for 30 minutes until puffed up and golden.

Using an oven glove, place a large plate over the pan and flip the tatin over - be careful as the caramel will be searing hot.

Serve with vanilla ice-cream.

# PUMPKIN PIE

SERVES 8-10

Prep time: 30 minutes
Chilling time: 30 minutes
Cooking time: 1 hour

*You will need a 25cm
round loose-bottomed tart tin
and some baking beans*

For the pastry case:
170g plain flour, plus
    extra for dusting
55g cold vegetable fat
30g cold butter

For the filling:
1 tin pumpkin purée
200ml double cream
3 eggs
100g golden caster sugar
2 teaspoons ground
    cinnamon
2 teaspoon ground ginger

whipped cream or ice-cream,
    to serve

I tried pumpkin pie with my girlfriends for the first time on Thanksgiving in 2015. We went to my friend Vanessa's house for dinner and I brought along some American offerings – one being an awesome wine called Boom Boom Syrah, the other being pumpkin pie. Most of us had not tried it before and didn't really know what to expect but it was so wholesome and yummy. We ate it with vanilla ice-cream, although Vanessa ran out and started offering mini Magnums. If you're British this may seem like a slightly strange recipe but please try it, it's absolutely heaven!

In a bowl, mix the flour, fat and butter with fingertips until crumbly.

Add 3 tablespoons of cold water to make a ball of pastry. Wrap in clingfilm and chill in the fridge for 30 minutes.

Preheat the oven for 190°C/375°F/GM5.

Thinly roll out your pastry on a floured work surface to 2–3mm thick and use it to line the tart tin, leaving the excess hanging off the edge. Gently press in the sides, then line the pastry with greaseproof paper and fill with baking beans. Bake for 10 minutes before removing the beans, pricking the base with a fork and baking for another 10 minutes until the pastry is golden and completely dry. Trim the excess pastry with a serrated knife to form a neat edge.

In a bowl, mix all the filling ingredients until smooth and light, then transfer to the case and bake for 40 minutes until golden but with a slight wobble in the centre.

Leave to cool slightly then transfer to a wire rack to cool completely, then serve with whipped cream or ice-cream.

Pecans always remind me of my mum as she's a huge fan of those maple and pecan plaits you get in bakeries, as well as pecan pie. It's not something she's ever made herself at home, so Mum, I hope you have fun making this.

# PECAN PIE

SERVES 8-10

Prep time: 20 minutes
Chilling time: 30 minutes
Cooking time: 40 minutes

*You will need a 25cm round loose-bottomed tart tin and some baking beans*

For the pastry case:
200g plain flour, plus
    extra for dusting
50g cold vegetable fat
50g cold butter

For the filling:
150g butter
250g soft brown sugar
150g golden syrup
3 eggs, beaten
1 teaspoon vanilla extract
pinch of salt
300g whole pecans

vanilla ice-cream or cream,
    to serve

Mix the flour, vegetable fat and butter between your fingers until you have the consistency of breadcrumbs. Add 3 tablespoons of water and combine to make a ball of pastry.

Roll out the pastry on a floured surface to a thickness of about 3–4mm, then transfer to a tart tin, pressing the edges and sides in gently. Leave the excess hanging off the sides and chill in the fridge for 30 minutes.

Preheat the oven to 180°C/350°F/GM4.

Line the pastry with greaseproof paper and fill with baking beans. Bake for 10 minutes before removing the beans, pricking the base with a fork and baking for another 10 minutes until the pastry is golden and completely dry.

To make the filling, melt the butter, sugar and golden syrup in a large saucepan, and put aside briefly to cool.

Whisk in the eggs, vanilla and salt until fully combined. Pour the mixture into the pastry case, arrange the pecans on top and bake for 30–40 minutes until golden brown. Don't worry if it has a wobble – the pie will set as it cools.

Leave to cool in the tin and serve with vanilla ice-cream or whipped cream.

My sister Tash has been obsessed with profiteroles her whole life, they are her favourite. Growing up, we always had to let her have the last one or she'd never let us forget it. So Tash, this recipe is dedicated to you!

# PROFITEROLES

MAKES ABOUT 20

Prep time: 30 minutes
Cooking time: 25 minutes

*You will need a piping bag with 1cm nozzle*

For the pastry:
100g unsalted butter
50g golden caster sugar
120g plain flour
4 eggs

To serve:
500ml double cream
100g dark chocolate
(70% cocoa solids)

Preheat the oven to 190°C/375°F/GM5. Line two baking trays with greaseproof paper and set aside.

Place 225ml water, the butter and sugar in a large saucepan and set over a low heat until the butter has melted. Turn up the heat and bring the mixture to a simmer. Take off the heat, quickly pour in the flour and immediately start beating until a smooth dough has formed. Set aside to cool.

Beat the eggs in a jug. Slowly add the eggs to the dough in small batches, beating the egg fully into the dough each time, until the dough is smooth, glossy and has a soft, dropping consistency – you may not need all the egg.

Transfer the dough to a piping bag with a 1cm nozzle, then pipe small balls onto the baking sheet, leaving space between each ball. Pat the top of each ball with a wet finger so that each ball is smooth.

Bake in the oven for 20–25 minutes until golden brown and risen. Switch off the oven. Pierce the bottom of each profiterole with a knife, and pop back in the oven for 2 minutes to release the steam from the middle, then transfer to a wire rack to cool.

In a bowl, whip the double cream until stiff peaks form, then transfer to a piping bag. Ease the nozzle inside the cut at the bottom of each profiterole, and pipe in the whipped cream until full.

Melt the chocolate in a bain marie, or in a bowl over a pan of simmering water. Arrange the profiteroles in a tower, drizzle the chocolate over and serve.

# SALTED CHOCOLATE TART

SERVES 8-10

Prep time: 20 minutes
Chilling time: at least 4 hours

*You will need a 25cm round loose-bottomed tart tin*

Ingredients:
350g bourbon biscuits
90g unsalted butter, melted
175g dark chocolate
(70% cocoa solids)
75g milk chocolate
350ml double cream
1 teaspoon vanilla paste
60g unsalted butter
1 teaspoon sea salt flakes
(or to taste), plus extra
for sprinkling

This is such a classic dessert, with its rich truffly filling, but I decided to make the base from one of my favourite chocolate biscuits, the bourbon. This decision resulted in the most divine transformation. You have to try it.

Blend the biscuits in a food processor until fine. Add the melted butter. Mix thoroughly until the butter is well dispersed and the biscuit holds its shape when pressed together between two fingers.

Tip the mixture into the tart tin, and gently but firmly press it against the base and sides to create the tart shell. Chill in the fridge for at least 2 hours, or overnight.

Break up the dark and milk chocolate into small pieces. Pour the double cream and vanilla into a pan and simmer over a medium heat, then take off just before it comes to a boil. Add the chocolates and butter. Leave to stand for 1 minute, then stir until combined, smooth and all the chocolate has melted.

Add the sea salt, stir well and pour the mixture into the tart tin. Gently shake the tin to allow the chocolate to settle evenly, then leave at room temperature to set for 2 hours.

Sprinkle some additional salt flakes on top to serve.

# BREAD

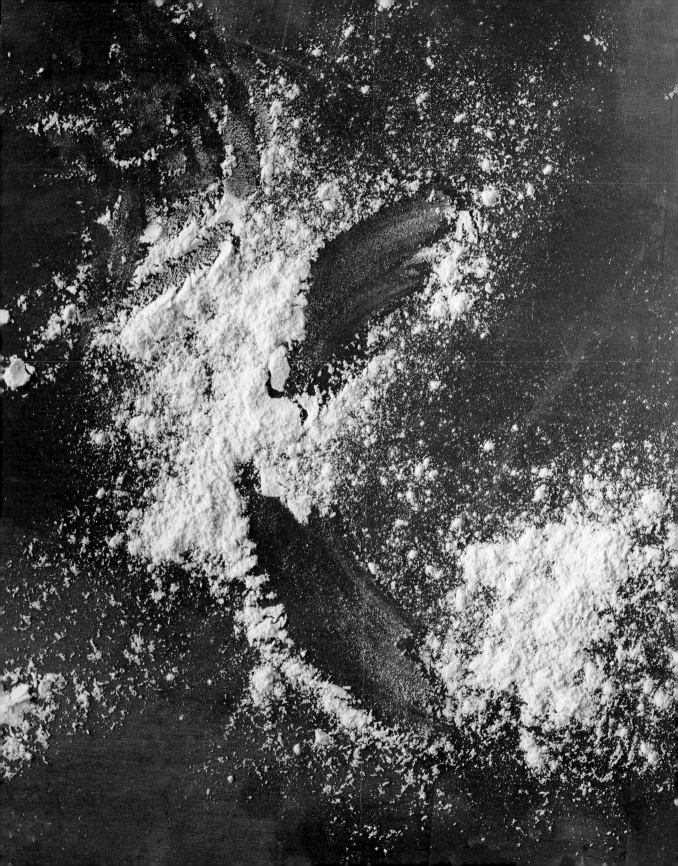

# "Happiness is freshly baked bread"

PRETZELS

DOUGHNUTS

CINNAMON BUNS

FRUIT SCONES

CHEESE SCONES

NUTELLA BUNS

ICED BUNS

FRYING PAN PIZZA

# PRETZELS

MAKES 12

Prep time: 20 minutes
Proving time: 1 hour
Baking time: 12 minutes

Ingredients:
500g strong white
    bread flour
1 x 7g sachet fast-action yeast
50g caster sugar
1 teaspoon salt
300ml warm milk
80g butter, melted
20g bicarbonate of soda
1 egg, beaten

To decorate:
1 tablespoon ground
    cinnamon
3 tablespoons golden
    caster sugar
sea salt flakes (optional)

New York is a place very close to my heart so I wanted to have a recipe here that reminded me of one of my favourite cities. If you've been to New York then you'll know that pretzels are pretty much on every street corner and are on every tourist's must-Instagram list. I've done a sweet and savoury version depending on what you fancy.

Put the flour, yeast, sugar and salt into a large bowl or mixer.

In a separate bowl, combine the milk and melted butter and slowly pour into the dry ingredients.

Bring together to form a dough, then knead for 10 minutes. Put in a greased bowl, cover with clingfilm and prove in a warm place for 1 hour, until doubled in size.

Preheat the oven to 200°C/400°F/GM6.

Split the dough into 12 pieces. Roll each out into a long thin sausage, about 40cm long.

Cross the ends of the dough twice, then bring the strands down and press into the dough.

Boil a full kettle, and pour into a large saucepan. Add the bicarbonate of soda (be careful – the water will fizz!) and mix until dissolved. Dunk each pretzel into the water for 10 seconds, removing with a slotted spoon. Transfer them to a baking tray.

Brush with the beaten egg. Combine the cinnamon and caster sugar and sprinkle over half the pretzels, and do sea salt on the others – whatever you fancy! Bake for 10–12 minutes, until golden.

# DOUGHNUTS

MAKES 12

Prep time: 10 minutes
Proving time: 1½ hours
Cooking time: 25 minutes

. . . . . . . . . . . .

Ingredients:
250g strong white
    bread flour, plus extra
    for dusting
30g caster sugar
1 teaspoon salt
1 x 7g sachet fast-action yeast
2 eggs
50g butter, melted
a large bottle of sunflower
    oil, for frying
jam, Nutella, ready-made
    custard, to fill

Until I started baking like crazy for this book and coming up with new recipes I had never actually made doughnuts at home before. The idea of making them seemed a bit scary but they are actually pretty straightforward. They take a little time, but they are so worth it and will taste better than any shop-bought variety. The fillings for these are inspired by the doughnuts I buy at my local market. I always find myself not knowing which flavour to go for – and I think the market lady can tell, as she oftens slips an extra doughnut into my bag.

. . . . . . . . . . . .

Put all the dough ingredients (minus the butter) into a mixer with 75ml water and whiz until almost combined, at this point pour in the melted butter and keep whizzing.

Once a dough has formed, knead on a floured surface until the dough becomes elastic. Leave in a bowl in a warm place to prove for 1 hour.

Knead the dough again, then split the mixture into 12 round pieces and arrange on a baking tray, leaving it to prove for a further 30 minutes.

Heat the oil in a deep pan until you can drop a piece of bread in and it sizzles.

Put the doughnuts, two at a time, into the oil and cook for around 1 minute on each side until golden. Remove from the oil and transfer to kitchen paper.

Roll the doughnuts in sugar and then, once cooled, make a slit in the side and pipe in your favourite filling – jam, Nutella, ready-made custard – there are plenty of options.

# CINNAMON BUNS

---●---

MAKES 12

. . . . . . . . . . . .

Prep time: 40 minutes
Proving time: 2½ hours
Cooking time: 30 minutes

. . . . . . . . . . . .

*You will need a 30 × 20cm baking tin*

Ingredients:
500g strong white bread
   flour, plus extra for
   dusting
pinch of salt
5 tablespoons golden
   caster sugar
2 x 7g sachets fast-action
   yeast
75g cold butter
2 eggs
1 tablespoon ground
   cinnamon

For the filling:
4 tablespoons soft brown
   sugar, plus extra for
   sprinkling
2 teaspoons ground
   cinnamon
100g butter, softened
large handful of raisins

For the icing:
100g icing sugar
½ teaspoon vanilla extract

Jim absolutely loves cinnamon buns. If ever we go to a bakery, they are the thing he always goes crazy for. In his words, they are 'sticky and delicious!'.

. . . . . . . . . . . .

Line the baking tin with greaseproof paper.

Mix the flour, salt and sugar in a bowl, stir in the yeast and rub in the butter.

Crack one of the eggs in the centre along with the milk, add the cinnamon and bring together to form a dough.

Turn out onto a floured surface and knead for 10 minutes until the dough is elastic.

Put in a bowl and allow to prove for about 1½ hours.

Meanwhile, you can make the filling by mixing the sugar, cinnamon and butter together in a bowl until it is soft and creamy.

When the dough has risen, knock the air out and roll into a large rectangle. Spread the cinnamon butter all over the dough right up to the corners. Sprinkle over the raisins evenly.

Roll up the dough and cut into 12 slices. Place each slice end up, side by side in the baking tin and allow to prove for another hour.

Preheat the oven to 180°C/350°F/GM4. Beat the other egg and use it as a wash over the buns. Bake for about 30 minutes.

Meanwhile, make the icing. Mix the sugar and vanilla and add 1 tablespoon of warm water slowly until you have your desired consistency, then pour over the buns.

# FRUIT SCONES

MAKES 10

Prep time: 20 minutes
Cooking time: 10–12 minutes

*You will need a 6cm
round cutter*

Ingredients:
250g self-raising flour,
    plus extra for dusting
50g golden caster sugar
½ teaspoon baking powder
100g cold unsalted butter
70g dried fruit
1 large egg, beaten
70ml milk, plus extra
    for brushing

To serve:
clotted cream and jam

I always used to make these at my grandparents'
house when I was little. My nanny used to bring
through one of the chairs from the dining room
to the kitchen so I could stand on it and reach the
counter top so we could make them together.
This is her recipe. I like to eat mine with loads
of cream and jam.

Preheat the oven to 200°C/400°F/GM6. Line
a baking sheet with greaseproof paper.

Sift the flour into a bowl and add the sugar and
baking powder. Rub the butter through with your
fingers to create a breadcrumb consistency.

Add the fruit and the beaten egg, and most of the
milk. Combine the ingredients together with a fork
to begin with, then use your hands to create a dough.
If it seems too dry, add the rest of the milk.

Turn the dough out onto a floured surface and roll
out to roughly 3cm thick. Cut out your scones with
a round cutter and transfer to the baking sheet.
Repeat until you've used up all the dough.

Brush the tops with a little milk, then bake for
10–12 minutes until golden. Allow to cool on
a wire rack, then serve with cream and jam.

# CHEESE SCONES

MAKES 10

Prep time: 20 minutes
Cooking time: 10–12 minutes

*You will need a 6cm
round cutter*

Ingredients:
250g self-raising flour,
   plus extra for dusting
½ teaspoon baking powder
½ teaspoon salt
50g cold unsalted
   butter, cubed
100g mature cheddar
1 large egg, beaten
100ml full-fat milk, plus
   extra for brushing

A great alternative to have on offer when you're making your fruit scones, as some people prefer savoury. I like to have one of each. You can eat your cheese scones spread with lots of soft butter straight from the oven whilst you wait for your fruit scones to cool down!

Preheat the oven to 200°C/400°F/GM6. Line a baking sheet with greaseproof paper.

Sift the flour, baking powder and salt into a large bowl and add the butter.

Rub the mixture between your fingers until the butter is well dispersed and has the consistency of breadcrumbs. Mix in the cheese, then add the beaten egg and milk.

Work the wet ingredients in with a fork, and then use your hands to form a dough.

Turn out on a floured surface, and roll out to a thickness of around 3cm. Use a cutter to cut out approximately 10 scones. You'll need to squash up and re-roll the dough as you go. Place the scones on the baking sheet and brush each with milk.

Bake for 10–12 minutes, until risen and golden on top.

# NUTELLA BUNS

Prep time: 40 minutes
Proving time: 2½ hours
Cooking time: 30 minutes

*You will need a 30 × 20cm baking tin*

Ingredients:
500g strong white bread
    flour, plus extra for dusting
pinch of sea salt
5 tablespoons golden
    caster sugar
2 x 7g sachets fast-action
    yeast
75g cold butter
2 eggs
300ml milk
200g Nutella

For the icing:
100g icing sugar
½ teaspoon vanilla extract

To serve:
100g toasted chopped
    hazelnuts

In the process of developing my cinnamon buns, I thought I'd try out a Nutella variation as I know there are a lot of Nutella fans out there. They worked a treat. I love watching them rise and puff up in the oven and then enjoying them as soon as they come out. These are a perfect Sunday morning treat.

. . . . . . . . . . . . .

Line the baking tin with greaseproof paper.

Mix the flour, salt and sugar in a bowl, stir in the yeast and rub in the butter.

Crack one of the eggs in the centre along with the milk and bring together to form a dough.

Turn out onto a floured surface and knead for 10 minutes until the dough is elastic. Put in a bowl and allow to prove for about 1½ hours.

When the dough has risen, knock out the air and roll into a large rectangle. Spread the Nutella all over the dough right up to the corners.

Roll up the dough and cut into 12 slices.

Place each slice end up, side by side in the baking tin and allow to prove for another hour.

Preheat the oven to 180°C/350°F/GM4. Beat the other egg and use it to glaze the buns. Bake for about 30 minutes.

Meanwhile, make the icing. Mix the sugar and vanilla and add 1 tablespoon of warm water slowly until you have your desired consistency, then pour over the buns.

Sprinkle with chopped hazelnuts and drizzle with the icing.

# ICED BUNS

MAKES 12

Prep time: 20 minutes
Cooking time: 10 minutes

Ingredients:
40g butter, plus extra
    for greasing
500g strong white
    bread flour, plus
    extra for dusting
2 x 7g sachets fast-action yeast
40g caster sugar
2 eggs
150ml warm milk

For the icing:
450g icing sugar

For the filling (optional):
whipped cream
strawberry jam

These, for me, were the ultimate school break-time snack. My friends and I used to rush to the front of the queue in the hope of getting the first iced buns. We'd then take them to our usual spot and catch up whilst we ate our sweet doughy treats.

. . . . . . . . . . . . .

Grease two baking trays.

Place all the dough ingredients in a bowl with 100ml water. Mix together with your hands until a dough forms, adding a little more water if needed.

Turn the dough out onto a floured surface and knead for 10 minutes, until the dough is springy and elastic. Return to a clean, greased bowl, cover with clingfilm and leave to prove for 1 hour in a warm place, until doubled in size.

Divide the dough into 12 pieces, and shape each into a long finger shape.

Put the buns onto the baking trays – six buns on each – and allow to prove for another hour, until doubled in size and touching.

Preheat the oven to 200°C/400°F/GM6.

Bake for 10 minutes until golden, transfer to a wire rack and leave to cool.

For the icing, sift the icing sugar into a bowl and add a tablespoon of water at a time until you get a thick icing. Dip the top of each bun into the bowl, allow the excess icing to drip off, then set aside to set slightly.

If you want to fill the buns, simply slice each in half and spoon in the whipped cream and a layer of jam.

# FRYING PAN PIZZA

Prep time: 10 minutes
Cooking time: 10 minutes
for each pizza

*You will need a non-stick frying pan*

Ingredients:
500g spelt flour, plus
    extra for dusting
1 teaspoon salt
1 jar tomato sauce
pizza topping of your
    choice, e.g. mozzarella,
    olives, salami, ham,
    pineapple, roasted
    vegetables, rocket etc.

These are the ultimate sleepover party pizzas. I love making these with my friends when they come to stay because they are quick, easy and fun to make and you can add whatever kind of toppings you like. I tend to organise a topping station and we all go to town on decorating our pizzas, coming up with different creations. On my pizza I like extra cheese (mozzarella and cheddar), ham and pineapple.

Mix the flour, 300ml cold water and salt in a food processor to form a dough.

Switch on the grill to a high setting. Put a non-stick frying pan over a high heat on the hob.

Divide the dough into four pieces and roll out each piece on a floured surface to form a circle.

Transfer one base to the frying pan. Fry on one side for 3 minutes, then flip it over and fry for another 3 minutes. While it's frying on its second side, spread a few tablespoons of tomato sauce over the top and add your toppings.

To finish, grill the pizza for 2–3 minutes, until the cheese has melted and your toppings have warmed through.

Repeat with the remaining dough, or refrigerate to use later. If serving the pizzas together, keep the cooked ones warm in the bottom of the oven, covered loosely in tin foil, until all are prepared.

# BRUNCH

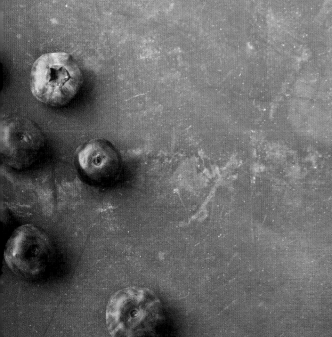

# "Pancakes in bed, please"

WAFFLES

FRENCH-STYLE PANCAKES

GRANOLA

CHEAT'S CROISSANTS & PAIN AU CHOCOLAT

FRENCH TOAST

POP-TARTS

JAMIE OLIVER'S AMERICAN STACK PANCAKES

CRUMPETS

# WAFFLES

MAKES 6

Prep time: 20 minutes
Proving time: 30 minutes
Cooking time: 10 minutes

. . . . . . . . . . . . .

*You will need a waffle griddle*

Ingredients:
100ml milk
1 tablespoon caster sugar
1 x 7g sachet fast-action
   yeast
300g strong white bread flour,
   plus extra for dusting
2 eggs
150g butter, melted
pinch of salt

For the honeycomb butter:
100g honeycomb
250g butter, softened

To serve (optional):
sliced banana
maple syrup
icing sugar

My favourite kind of waffles are the ones sold at the Ben and Jerry's counter in the cinema – dense, slightly chewy and sweet. When I first tried making them at home, they were almost like pancakes in the shape of waffles and nothing like the awesome ones at the cinema. I played around with the recipe a few times and have ended up with a pretty close match; these taste even better because they are home-made.

. . . . . . . . . . . . .

First prepare the honeycomb butter. Crush the honeycomb into small pieces and mix thoroughly into the softened butter. Once evenly combined, lay on top of a sheet of clingfilm, then roll up into a sausage shape and pop in the fridge – you will be able to cut slices off it once it has set.

For the waffles, warm the milk, add the sugar and yeast, stir well and set aside.

Sift the flour into a large bowl and add the milk mixture, eggs and most of the melted butter, reserving some for brushing the iron later. Mix fully to form a smooth dough. Cover with clingfilm and leave for 30 minutes.

Turn out onto a floured surface and knead for 5 minutes.

Divide the dough into 6 palm-sized pieces, flattening them out to fit your griddle size.

Heat up the waffle iron and brush with the remaining melted butter. Place the waffle pieces onto the iron and cook for 2 minutes on each side until puffed up and golden.

Transfer to a plate. If desired, top with sliced banana, a slice of honeycomb butter, maple syrup and/or a sprinkling of icing sugar.

# FRENCH-STYLE PANCAKES
## (CREPES)

MAKES ABOUT 6

Prep time: 5 minutes
Cooking time: 15 minutes

. . . . . . . . . . . . . .

Ingredients:
100g plain flour
2 eggs
250ml full-fat milk
knob of butter, plus extra
    for frying

To serve:
caster sugar
lemon wedges

If it snowed heavily, our school would close for the day – what we called a snow day. On snow days, my friends would come to mine as my mum was a childminder so was used to having a house-full. We would get the duvet down from my bedroom and snuggle on the sofa and watch our favourite Disney films, drink warm orange squash and eat pancakes. We made the thin kind that are really like French crepes, but in the UK we just call them pancakes. I have always had mine with sugar and lemon but the options for toppings are endless. Whenever I make these, it reminds me of snow days with my friends and brings back so many happy memories.

. . . . . . . . . . . . .

Put the flour in a large bowl. Crack in the eggs and whisk well. Slowly add the milk until you have a smooth and very runny batter.

Put a pan on high heat and melt a big knob of butter, once melted pour it into your batter mixture and stir through. Reintroduce a little more melted butter into the pan each time you pour one ladle of batter in, and use the ladle to spread it evenly.

Fry for 2 minutes, then flip over to cook the other side. Repeat the process, keeping the cooked pancakes in a warmed oven.

For the classic pancake, serve sprinkled with sugar and freshly-squeezed lemon juice; though the options are of course endless, both sweet and savoury.

# GRANOLA

MAKES LOADS
(ABOUT 1.1KG)

Prep time: 5 minutes
Cooking time: 10–15 minutes

Ingredients:
250ml runny honey
5 tablespoons coconut oil
50g pumpkin seeds
50g flax seeds
200g almonds, roughly
  chopped
500g rolled oats
200g dried apricots, chopped

To serve:
milk or yoghurt
berries

I absolutely love having a jar of homemade granola in my kitchen as a healthy breakfast option. I eat it with milk or with yoghurt and fruit. I've made lots of different granolas over the years and this is my favourite mixture. I love all the textures and knowing where every ingredient has come from gives it a really wholesome feeling.

Preheat the oven to 180°C/350°F/GM4. Line two baking trays with greaseproof paper.

Melt the honey and coconut oil in a pan until runny and combined.

Add everything but the dried apricots to a large bowl, pour over the honey mix and stir together until everything is well coated.

Spread evenly across the baking trays and bake for 10–15 minutes until toasted and golden.

Stir through the chopped apricots and allow to cool.

Transfer to an airtight containe. The granola will keep for up to a month.

Serve with berries and milk or yoghurt.

# CHEAT'S CROISSANTS & PAIN AU CHOCOLAT

MAKES 8

Prep time: 15 minutes
Cooking time: 15 minutes

Ingredients:
1 ready-rolled all-butter puff
   pastry sheet, at room
   temperature
75g milk chocolate chips
1 egg, beaten

A breakfast table classic. These are really nice to make if you have friends to stay. They make breakfast in the morning a little bit special.

Preheat the oven to 200°C/400°F/GM6. Line a baking tray with greaseproof paper.

Unroll the pastry and cut the sheet into four squares. Cut each square in half so that you have triangles.

To roll the croissant, take a bottom corner of the pastry and roll it towards the longer, pointed end. Don't roll too tightly or the pastry won't puff up properly. Curl the ends down into the shape of a croissant.

To make pain au chocolat, sprinkle a small handful of chocolate chips at the bottom of the pastry, before you start rolling, and roll it up with you as you go.

Transfer to the baking tray and brush with the beaten egg. Bake for 15 minutes until puffed up and golden.

# FRENCH TOAST

### SERVES 1

Prep time: 10 minutes
Cooking time: 10 minutes

Ingredients:
50g blueberries
50g raspberries
1½ tablespoons icing sugar
50g mascarpone
1 extra-thick slice of
    white bread
2 eggs
pinch of ground cinnamon
knob of butter

To serve:
raspberry coulis
icing sugar
mint leaves

This recipe is inspired by the best French toast I have ever eaten, at Gemma at The Bowery Hotel in New York. Berries, mascarpone-filled thick-cut bread, dipped in maple syrup, it's a pretty magical breakfast.

Prepare the coulis by popping the berries in a saucepan over a medium heat. Stir in a tablespoon of the icing sugar and stir until the berries start to break down. Keep warm.

Mix the mascarpone with the remaining ½ tablespoon of icing sugar until smooth.

Slice a deep cut into the side of your bread and insert the mascarpone filling.

In a shallow dish, whisk the eggs with the cinnamon, and dip the bread in on both sides, allowing the bread to soak up as much egg as possible.

Heat a knob of butter in a frying pan over high heat. Once melted, drop in the eggy bread. Fry on both sides until crispy and golden, then transfer to a plate, cut in half.

Serve with the raspberry coulis, a sprinkling of icing sugar and mint leaves.

# POP-TARTS

Prep time: 40 minutes
Cooking time: 20–25 minutes

Ingredients:
250g plain flour
2 tablespoons golden
    caster sugar
1 teaspoon salt
200g cold butter
1 egg, plus extra for brushing
1 tablespoon milk

For the filling:
½ jar (225g) strawberry jam
1 tablespoon cornflour

To decorate:
200g icing sugar
pink food colouring
sugar strands
ready-made strawberry
    sauce (optional)

Growing up, I'd never eaten a Pop-Tart. However, when I first met my friend Zoe she was going through a big Pop-Tart phase and said I must try one at once. I loved the concept of it and the fun flavours that were available but I didn't rate the taste all that much. I'd seen online people had made their own so I decided to have a go, too. I went for the classic strawberry jam flavour, which tastes delicious warm and I think the icing looks so cute. Zoe, I dedicate this recipe to you.

Preheat the oven to 180°C/350°F/GM4. Line 2 baking trays with greaseproof paper.

To make the dough, mix the flour, sugar and salt in a bowl, then rub in the butter with your fingertips to a breadcrumb consistency. Mix in the egg and a tablespoon of milk until a dough forms – add a little more milk if it's looking too dry.

Heat the jam and cornflour over a low heat until it's loosened. Set aside to cool slightly.

Roll out the dough to 3mm thick. Cut the dough into 8cm x 14cm rectangles – you should get at least 12 rectangles.

To assemble, lay out six rectangles on the baking trays. Add a teaspoon or two of the jam filling to each square, leaving a centimetre around the edge. Brush the edge with egg and lay the remaining pastry rectangles over the top. Use a fork to press down around the edges, then poke a hole in the top of each one. Brush each tart with egg and bake for 20–25 minutes until golden. Transfer to a wire rack to cool.

To decorate, combine the icing sugar, food colouring and a little water in a bowl until you have a thick icing.

Spread a layer of icing over each tart and sprinkle with the sugar strands. Drizzle with strawberry sauce if desired.

# JAMIE OLIVER'S AMERICAN STACK PANCAKES

### SERVES 2 GENEROUSLY

Prep time: 10 minutes
Cooking time: 15 minutes

Ingredients:
3 large eggs
115g plain flour
1 heaped teaspoon
   baking powder
140ml milk
pinch of salt
knob of butter

To serve:
knob of butter
mixed berries
maple syrup

I have learned lots of tricks and tips from Jamie Oliver over the years, as I'm sure a lot of us have, and I've also had the pleasure of getting to know him as a friend, too. His American pancake recipe really is the best so here's my take on it. It does take some time whipping up the eggs, but think of the muscles you'll build up in the process!

Separate the eggs between two large bowls. Add the flour, baking powder and milk to the yolks and mix to form a smooth, thick batter.

In a clean dry bowl, whisk the whites with the salt until soft peaks form and fold into the batter with a metal spoon.

Heat a non-stick frying pan over a medium heat and melt the knob of butter. Pour a heaped tablespoon of batter into the pan – you can probably fit three heaped tablespoons at a time. Fry for 2 minutes until air bubbles rise to the surface, then flip over. The pancakes are ready when they're golden and firm on both sides. Keep the cooked pancakes warm in the oven, and repeat the process until you've used up all the batter.

Stack the pancakes on a plate and serve with a knob of butter, berries and maple syrup.

# CRUMPETS

MAKES 10-12

Prep time: 25 minutes
Proving time: 1 hour

*4 chef's rings/crumpet rings*

300ml full-fat milk
250g strong white
    bread flour
1 x 7g sachet fast-action
    yeast
½ teaspoon bicarbonate
    of soda
1 teaspoon salt
1 teaspoon caster sugar
butter, for brushing,
    cooking and to serve

I love crumpets, and until recently I didn't imagine they could be so easy to make at home, but they really are! It's so satisfying to see the bubbles forming as they're being fried – I really recommend giving them a go. Perfect for a sunny Saturday morning.

Put the milk and 80ml water in a saucepan and heat until warm - you should be able to comfortably leave your finger in.

Mix the flour, yeast, bicarbonate of soda, salt and caster sugar in a large bowl and make a well in the centre. Pour in the warm milk and whisk together until well combined - be careful not to overwork the batter.

Cover with a clean tea towel and leave in a warm place for 40 minutes-1 hour, until doubled in size and bubbly.

Brush the insides of the chef's rings with melted butter. Place a heavy-bottomed frying pan on a medium flame and brush with melted butter.

Place the rings on the frying pan, and spoon three tablespoons of batter into each ring. Turn the heat down to low and cook for 10 minutes - bubbles will form and pop on the surface of your crumpet and it should be almost cooked through.

Remove the chef's rings (be careful as they'll be hot) and flip the crumpets over. Cook for another 2 minutes or until golden.

Set the crumpets aside on a lined baking sheet and repeat the process until all the batter has been used.

To serve, heat the crumpets in a preheated oven at 150°C/300°F/GM2 for 10 minutes, or toast one at a time in a toaster and serve with plenty of butter.

# SPECIAL OCCASIONS

# "Make a wish"

FESTIVE YULE LOG

REINDEER COOKIES

MINCE PIES

SALTED CHOCOLATE TRUFFLES

EDIBLE CHRISTMAS TREE DECORATIONS

PUMPKIN POPS

SKELETON BISCUITS

CHOCOLATE FUDGE SPIDER-WEB CAKE

HALLOWEEN CUPCAKES

HOT CROSS BUNS

EASTER NESTS

PRETTY YELLOW BIG EASTER CAKE

BIRTHDAY CAKE

BIRTHDAY CUPCAKES

ULTIMATE CELEBRATION CAKE

# FESTIVE YULE LOG

SERVES 10-12

Prep time: 20 minutes
Cooking time: 10 minutes

*You will need a Swiss roll tin*

Ingredients:
4 large eggs
140g golden caster sugar
60g self-raising flour
50g cocoa powder
200ml double cream

For the ganache:
250ml double cream
250g dark chocolate,
    chopped

To decorate:
icing sugar, holly sprig
    and chocolate shavings

This is a great alternative to a traditional Christmas cake. It's really fun to make and you can add your personal Christmas touches to it. I love making mine look as log-like as possible and putting snow on top. It's a real crowd pleaser.

Preheat the oven to 200°C/400°F/GM6. Line a Swiss roll tin with greaseproof paper.

Whisk the eggs and sugar together until light and frothy. Sift the flour and cocoa powder into the eggs and mix until smooth and combined. Pour into the Swiss roll tin and bake for 8–10 minutes.

Turn the cake out onto a clean piece of greaseproof paper and unpeel the paper from its bottom.

Score a shallow line 2cm from the bottom of the sponge, taking care not to cut all the way through. Roll up the cake tightly, starting from the scored bottom. Leave to cool completely in this position.

While the sponge is cooling, make the ganache. Heat the cream in a saucepan until it starts to bubble at the edges. Take off the heat and add the chocolate, stirring until it is fully melted. Leave to cool completely.

For the filling, whip the double cream to soft peaks. Unroll the sponge carefully, then spread the cream over it evenly.

Carefully roll the sponge up again as tightly as possible and rest with the crease at the bottom.

Spread the ganache over the roll with a palette knife, making lines with a fork to resemble bark. Finish with a sprinkle of icing sugar and a few sprigs of holly. You can scatter chocolate shavings at the base of the log, too, to represent peeled bark.

# REINDEER COOKIES

MAKES 10

Prep time: 30 minutes
Cooking time: 10 minutes

Ingredients:
250g butter, softened
150g golden caster sugar
1 egg
2 teaspoons vanilla paste
350g plain flour, plus
    extra for dusting
½ teaspoon bicarbonate
    of soda

To decorate:
red Smarties
chocolate chips
chocolate-covered pretzels
icing sugar

It's always fun to make something super cute and festive at Christmas time. These little reindeer biscuits are loved by everyone in my family from the littlest ones to my grandparents.

Preheat the oven to 180°C/350°F/GM4. Line two baking trays with greaseproof paper.

Cream together the butter and sugar until light and fluffy, add the egg and vanilla paste, then mix in the flour and bicarbonate of soda to form a dough.

Roll out the dough on a floured surface to ½cm thick. Use a knife to cut out a 'blunted' triangular shape to form the reindeer's head. Transfer the cookie to one of the baking trays and repeat until all the dough has been used. Bake for 10–12 minutes until golden.

While still warm, press a red Smartie at the bottom for the nose, followed by two chocolate chips for the eyes and two chocolate pretzels to form antlers. Dust with icing sugar for a snowy effect.

# MINCE PIES

MAKES 12

Prep time: 20 minutes
Cooking time: 20 minutes

*You will need a 12-hole cupcake/muffin tray*

Ingredients:
60g cold butter, plus
    extra for greasing
340g plain flour, plus
    extra for dusting
110g cold vegetable fat
350g mincemeat
splash of full-fat milk
icing sugar, to dust

In my opinion, it's not Christmas without eating a mince pie or 12. They are so simple to make and in my family it's a festive tradition to make them. I like eating them warm, straight from the oven, with plenty of clotted cream or brandy butter sandwiched into the middle.

Preheat your oven to 200°C/400°F/GM6. Lightly grease the cupcake/muffin tray.

Mix the flour, fat and butter between your fingers until crumbly. Add 6 tablespoons of water and combine to make a ball of pastry.

Roll out on a floured surface to a thickness of about 3–4mm. Use a fluted round pastry cutter to cut 12 circles, each big enough to fit the holes in the tray.

Press the pastry firmly down into each hole and fill with a heaped teaspoon of mincemeat.

Cut out a further 12 circles to fit over the top of each pie, or use a festive cutter such as a star or christmas tree to form the lid.

Using a pastry brush, brush the milk over the exposed pastry. Bake in the oven for 20 minutes or until golden brown. Transfer to a wire rack to cool.

Dust with icing sugar, and enjoy!

# SALTED CHOCOLATE TRUFFLES

MAKES 20

Prep time: 10 minutes
Chilling time: 2 hours

Ingredients:
300ml double cream
300g dark chocolate
    (70% cocoa solids)
knob of butter
1 teaspoon sea salt

To decorate:
cocoa powder
chopped hazelnuts
chopped pistachios
edible gold glitter
popping candy
freeze-dried raspberries,
    finely chopped
dessicated coconut
ground coffee beans
hundreds and thousands

Anything salty and sweet makes me really excited. These truffles are great for dinner parties as an after-dinner treat or make a lovely gift if you box them up. If you don't eat them all in one go, then these also freeze well – just defrost them when you need them.

Heat the cream over a medium heat in a pan until bubbles begin to form at the sides.

Whilst this is heating, break the chocolate up into small pieces and put into a large bowl.

When the cream is ready, add the knob of butter and stir until dissolved.

Pour the hot mixture over the chocolate and stir until melted. Add the salt and mix through, then put in the fridge for at least 2 hours.

About 30 minutes before you are ready to make your truffles, take the mixture out of the fridge to warm slightly.

Pop all your preferred toppings into separate bowls and have a plate at the ready to put the truffles onto.

Use a teaspoon to scoop up the chocolate and use your hands to form into 2cm balls. Roll them in your topping of choice and ensure each is fully coated, then add to the plate.

Refrigerate until needed.

# EDIBLE CHRISTMAS TREE DECORATIONS

## MAKES 40

Prep time: 15 minutes
Cooking time: 10 minutes

. . . . . . . . . . . . . .

*You will need Christmas cookie cutters, ribbon or string and a piping bag with a fine nozzle*

Ingredients:
150g unsalted butter, softened
150g dark muscovado sugar
2 eggs
3 tablespoons golden syrup
400g plain flour, plus extra for dusting
1 teaspoon baking powder
1½ teaspoons ground cinnamon
½ teaspoon ground nutmeg
½ teaspoon ground ginger

For the icing:
200g icing sugar
1 teaspoon vanilla extract

When I was little we always had treats to eat on the tree. We'd always try to make them last all Christmas but they never did – we used to eat the chocolates and then put the foil back on the tree hoping that Mum wouldn't notice. These edible biscuits bring back memories of that time. See how long you can make yours last!

. . . . . . . . . . . . . .

Preheat the oven to 180°C/350°F/GM4. Line 2 baking trays with greaseproof paper.

Cream together the butter and sugar until light and fluffy. Add the eggs and golden syrup and combine well, then mix in the flour, baking powder and spices to make a smooth dough.

Roll out the dough on a floured surface to the width of about 3–4mm. Cut out with Christmas cookie cutters of your choice, and keep going until you've used up all the dough, arranging them on the baking trays as you go. Using a straw, poke out a hole in each biscuit.

Bake for 10–12 minutes until golden. While the biscuits are still hot, poke through each hole with the straw again as some will have closed while baking. Transfer to a wire rack and leave to cool completely.

Mix 1 tablespoon of warm water at a time into the icing sugar, until you have a thick, pipeable icing. Transfer to a piping bag with your thinnest nozzle, and decorate your cookies.

When the icing is set, string a ribbon or string through each hole and hang on your tree.

# PUMPKIN POPS

Prep time: 40 minutes
Cooking time: 20 minutes
Cooling time: 1 hour

*You will need lolly sticks/
skewers and a 21cm round
loose-bottomed cake tin*

Ingredients:
200g plain flour
150g soft light brown sugar
1½ teaspoons baking powder
1 teaspoon ground cinnamon
1 teaspoon ground ginger
pinch of ground nutmeg
90ml full-fat milk
1 egg
100g pumpkin purée
100g unsalted butter, melted

For the icing:
50g butter, softened
100g icing sugar
50g cream cheese

To decorate:
200g white chocolate
edible gold glitter
Halloween decorations

My friend Maddie's mum is the queen of cake pops. She made an enormous batch for my very first Tanya Burr Cosmetics launch party. It was the first time I had ever had a cake pop and I wanted to eat about 10, they were so delicious! Cake pops are incredibly moist because you are mixing butter icing in with the cake crumbs to create little balls of squishy cake heaven. I made these pumpkin pops last Halloween, they were so cute that it was a struggle not to Instagram them! But obviously, I had to keep them secret for the book.

Preheat the oven to 180°C/350°F/GM4. Grease and line the cake tin.

Put the dry ingredients in a large bowl.

Add the milk and egg and mix, followed by the pumpkin purée and butter. Combine to form a smooth batter, then transfer to the cake tin and bake for 20 minutes. Transfer to a wire rack to cool.

Once cooled, crumble the cake into fine crumbs.

For the icing, in a bowl beat the butter and icing sugar until smooth and light, then fold in the cream cheese. Stir in the cake crumbs until fully mixed.

Roll the mixture into small balls, place on a baking sheet and refrigerate for 1 hour.

Melt the white chocolate in a bain marie or over a pan of simmering water. Put a skewer or lolly stick into each cake ball and dip into the melted white chocolate, allowing the excess to drip off.

Dip the ball into your desired toppings, then leave to stand until set.

# SKELETON
# BISCUITS

MAKES LOTS!
(MY CUTTER SIZE
MADE 18 BISCUITS)

Prep time: 20 minutes
Chilling time: 30 minutes
Cooking time: 15 minutes

* * * * * * * * * * *

*You will need a gingerbread
man cookie cutter and piping
bag with fine nozzle*

Ingredients:
200g unsalted butter,
    softened
200g soft light brown sugar
1 large egg
3 tablespoons golden syrup
400g plain flour, plus extra
    for dusting
60g cocoa powder
1 teaspoon baking powder

To decorate:
200g icing sugar

I was searching on Pinterest last Halloween for fun things to make and came across so many cute photos of skeleton biscuits. I thought the chocolate ones looked the coolest because of the contrast of the dark biscuit against the white icing. You can really get creative with your decorating and show off your icing skills. Try some witches and spider shapes as well as skeletons.

In a bowl, cream together the butter and sugar. Add the egg and golden syrup, then mix in the flour, cocoa and baking powder to form a dough.

Shape into a ball, wrap in clingfilm and chill in the fridge for 30 minutes.

Preheat the oven to 170°C/325°F/GM3. Line three baking trays with greaseproof paper.

Roll out the dough on a floured surface to ½cm thick – you may want to do this in batches. Use your gingerbread man cutter to cut out shapes until all the dough has been used up.

Place them on the baking trays and bake for around 15 minutes, or until golden.

Transfer to a wire rack to cool completely.

Mix 1 tablespoon of warm water into your icing sugar at a time, until it is thick and not too runny. Transfer to a piping bag and pipe skeletons onto the cooled biscuits.

# CHOCOLATE FUDGE SPIDER-WEB CAKE

### SERVES 8-10

Prep time: 40 minutes
Cooking time: 30 minutes
Cooling time: 10 minutes

*You will need 2 × 21cm round loose-bottomed cake tins*

Ingredients:
200g dark chocolate
   (70% cocoa solids)
200g unsalted butter
250g plain flour
50g cocoa powder
1 teaspoon bicarbonate
   of soda
2 teaspoons baking powder
200g dark muscovado sugar
200ml buttermilk
3 eggs

For the icing:
200g dark chocolate
250g slightly salted butter,
   softened
275g icing sugar
1 teaspoon vanilla extract
½ bar (25g) white chocolate

To decorate:
a spider, edible or not

This is the ultimate indulgent chocolate fudge cake, it's gooey, super chocolatey and a perfectly creepy Halloween centrepiece.

Preheat the oven to 180°C/350°F/GM4. Grease and line two cake tins.

Melt the chocolate and butter in a saucepan until smooth. Set aside to cool slightly.

Sift the flour, cocoa powder, bicarbonate of soda and baking powder into a large bowl and add the muscovado sugar.

Mix together the buttermilk and eggs in a separate bowl and add the chocolate mixture. Fold in the flour to form a smooth batter and divide between the two cake tins.

Bake for 30 minutes, then leave to cool in the tin.

For the icing, melt the dark chocolate in a bowl set over simmering water, making sure the bottom of the bowl doesn't touch the water. Set aside to cool slightly.

Cream the butter in a bowl until light and smooth, then slowly add the icing sugar until fully incorporated. Add the dark chocolate and vanilla to form a smooth icing.

Melt the white chocolate in the same way, then transfer to a piping bag with a thin nozzle and leave to cool for 10 minutes until slightly cooled.

Use about half the mixture to sandwich the cake together, then use the rest to ice the top and sides of the cake. Pipe even circles on top, starting in the middle and working outwards. Use a skewer to draw lines from the centre to the edge of the cake, to create a spider web. Pop a decorative spider on top and enjoy!

# HALLOWEEN CUPCAKES

MAKES 12

Prep time: 25 minutes
Cooking time: 15 minutes

*You will need a 12-hole cupcake/muffin tray*

Ingredients:
50g unsalted butter, softened
180g caster sugar
100g plain flour
60g cocoa powder
2 teaspoons baking powder
160ml milk
1 egg
½ teaspoon vanilla extract
100g chocolate chips

For the icing:
250g unsalted butter,
    softened
500g icing sugar
½ teaspoon vanilla extract
2 x Dr. Oetker orange
    gel colouring

To decorate:
raspberry jam
Halloween-themed sweets

As a huge fan of any vampire-related books, films or TV shows I wanted to create a cupcake recipe for Halloween that was slightly gory. I posted this recipe on my YouTube channel and so many people enjoyed making them at home that I had to put them in the book. It's fun seeing your friends' faces when you offer them a blood-filled cupcake.

Preheat the oven to 180°C/350°F/GM4 and line the cupcake/muffin tray with paper cases.

In a bowl, cream together the butter and sugar until light and fluffy.

Fold in the flour, cocoa powder and baking powder, then slowly add the milk, mixing as you go.

Crack in the egg, add the vanilla extract and beat until smooth before adding the chocolate chips.

Spoon the mixture evenly between the cupcake cases, and bake for 15 minutes until springy to touch. Transfer to a wire rack to cool.

Once cool, make the icing. In a bowl, combine all icing the ingredients until smooth and consistent.

Make a hole in the middle of each cupcake and fill with jam.

Pipe or spoon the icing on top of each cupcake, and decorate with your favourite Halloween treats.

# HOT CROSS BUNS

MAKES 12

Prep time: 30 minutes
Proving time: 2 hours
Cooking time: 15 minutes

Ingredients:
50g butter
150ml full-fat milk
50g caster sugar
zest of 1 orange
400g strong white bread
    flour, plus extra for
    dusting
1 x 7g sachet fast-action
    yeast
100g raisins or mixed
    dried fruit
2 teaspoons mixed spice
2 eggs, 1 to make an
    egg wash

For the cross:
6 tablespoons plain flour

For the sugar glaze:
25g caster sugar

I love hot cross buns so much! I actually eat them all year round, and I love making them at home. They smell so good in the oven and there is something so rewarding about making them with your own hands rather than settling for shop-bought.

Line a baking tray with greaseproof paper.

In a pan, melt together the butter, milk, caster sugar and orange zest. Set aside.

In a separate bowl, mix together the flour, yeast, raisins and mixed spice. Pour in the warm milky mixture, followed by the egg, and combine to form a sticky dough.

On a floured surface, knead by hand for 10 minutes until you have an elastic dough. Form into a ball and place in a lightly-oiled bowl. Cover with a tea towel for 1 hour, or until doubled in size.

Knock the dough back and split into 12 balls, shaping into round buns.

Put on the baking tray and don't worry if they touch – it'll create a nice tearing effect. Cover with clingfilm and allow to prove again for another hour, until the buns have risen again.

Preheat the oven to 200°C/400°F/GM6.

Make an egg wash by whisking one egg with 1 teaspoon of water. Brush the risen buns with the egg wash. Then for the cross, combine the flour with 2 tablespoons of water. If it looks too runny, add a little more flour. Transfer to a piping bag and pipe a cross onto each bun.

Bake for 15 minutes, or until golden. While the buns are in the oven, prepare the sugar glaze by melting the sugar in 20ml boiling water.

Brush the glaze on as soon as the buns are out of the oven, and enjoy with plenty of butter.

# EASTER NESTS

MAKES 12

Prep time: 20 minutes

*You will need a 12-hole cupcake/muffin tray*

Ingredients:
400g milk chocolate
50g unsalted butter
200g bite-size shredded
   wheat
2 bags of mini eggs

These are so easy and fun to make. I love making them with the little children in my family as they are something I made every Easter, without fail, when I was small. If you don't like shredded wheat, you could use Rice Krispies or cornflakes instead, which both work great.

Line the cupcake/muffin tray with paper cases.

Melt the chocolate and butter in a bowl set over a pan of simmering water, making sure the bottom of the bowl doesn't touch the water.

Break up the shredded wheat, then add this to the chocolate mixture and stir well until combined.

Divide the mixture between the paper cases, pressing down to create a dip in the middle of each nest.

Add three mini eggs to each nest and allow to cool before eating.

# PRETTY YELLOW BIG EASTER CAKE

SERVES 8-10

Prep time: 45 minutes
Cooking time: 20 minutes
Chilling time: 30 minutes

*You will need 3 × 21cm round loose-bottomed cake tins*

Ingredients:
200g white chocolate
300g butter, softened
300g golden caster sugar
4 eggs
350g plain flour
1½ teaspoon bicarbonate
   of soda
1½ teaspoons baking powder
½ teaspoon salt
200ml buttermilk

For the icing:
300g butter, softened
600g icing sugar
1 teaspoon vanilla essence
yellow food colouring

To decorate:
chocolate mini eggs and
   a white chocolate bunny

This is the perfect cake to make for Easter Sunday when all the family is around and everyone has overdone it on the chocolate. The sunshine yellow frosting makes it look so beautiful laid out on an Easter table for some afternoon tea.

Preheat the oven to 180°C/350°F/GM4. Grease and line the cake tins.

Melt the white chocolate in a bowl set over a pan of simmering water, making sure the bottom of the bowl doesn't touch the water.

Cream together the butter and sugar until pale and fluffy. Mix in the eggs, followed by the flour, bicarbonate of soda, baking powder and salt. Add the buttermilk and melted white chocolate, and mix to form a smooth, silky batter.

Divide between the cake tins and spread the batter out slightly with a spatula.

Bake for 20 minutes, or until the cakes are golden and risen. Leave to cool.

Make the icing by creaming the butter, and slowly adding the icing sugar until smooth and light. Add the vanilla essence. Then add a few drops of yellow food colouring at a time until you have a shade of yellow to your liking.

Sandwich the cakes together with the icing, then spread a very thin layer around the top and outside to catch the crumbs.

Chill in the fridge for 30 minutes to set the icing slightly, then use the remaining icing to fully cover the cake. Decorate with mini eggs and a white chocolate bunny.

# BIRTHDAY CAKE

SERVES 8-10

Prep time: 20 minutes
Cooking time: 20 minutes

*You will need 3 × 21cm round loose-bottomed cake tins*

Ingredients:
330g unsalted butter, softened
330g golden caster sugar
4 eggs
330g self-raising flour
1 teaspoon baking powder
1 teaspoon vanilla extract
splash of milk

For the icing:
250g unsalted butter, softened
450g icing sugar, plus extra to dust
pink food colouring

To decorate:
sprinkles and candles

This is what I call the Pinterest birthday cake. Everyone will want to get lots of photos before taking a slice. These colours just say birthday to me! This cake looks really beautiful with just simple pink stripy candles, but it's also fun to add singing candles, sparklers and fountain candles for extra birthday sparkle!

Preheat the oven to 180°C/350°F/GM4. Grease and line the cake tins.

In a bowl, cream together the butter and sugar until light and fluffy. Mix in the eggs, then add the flour, baking powder, vanilla and a small splash of milk to form a smooth batter.

Divide between the three tins and bake for 20 minutes. Leave to cool.

For the icing, cream the butter, then slowly add the sifted icing sugar until fully incorporated and smooth. Gradually add the pink food colouring until it's as vibrant as you like.

Sandwich the cake together with the icing, then spread the rest all over the cake. Dust the top with icing sugar and decorate with any celebratory toppings you wish!

# BIRTHDAY CUPCAKES

MAKES 12

Prep time: 15 minutes
Cooking time: 20 minutes

. . . . . . . . . . . . .

*You will need a 12-hole cupcake/muffin tray*

Ingredients:
50g butter, softened
180g caster sugar
160g plain flour
2 teaspoons baking powder
160ml milk
1 egg
splash of vanilla extract

For the icing:
500g icing sugar
250g butter, softened
½ teaspoon vanilla extract
3 food colourings of
    your choice

I think these are the sweetest cupcakes and I love making them for my friends and family on their birthdays. They are really straightforward, but what makes them that little bit special is the multicoloured icing.

. . . . . . . . . . . . .

Preheat the oven to 180C/350°F/GM4. Line the cupcake/muffin tray with paper cases.

Cream together the butter and sugar until light and fluffy. Fold in the flour and baking powder and slowly add the milk.

Crack in the egg and add the vanilla extract. Beat to a smooth consistency.

Spoon the mixture into the paper cases and bake for 20 minutes. Cool slightly in the tin then transfer to a wire rack to cool completely.

For the icing, mix together the icing sugar, butter and vanilla extract to form a smooth, light icing. Spoon into 3 separate bowls, then add to each your food colourings of choice, maybe even two-tone, and pipe onto the cold cupcakes.

# ULTIMATE CELEBRATION CAKE

## SERVES 8-10

Prep time: 45 minutes
Cooking time: 20 minutes

· · · · · · · · · · · · ·

*You will need 3 × 21cm round loose-bottomed cake tins*

Ingredients:
150ml full-fat milk
3 tablespoons black treacle
150g dark chocolate
  (70% cocoa solids)
275g plain flour
75g light soft brown sugar
150g cocoa powder
3 teaspoons baking powder
2 teaspoons bicarbonate
  of soda
3 large eggs
300ml Greek yoghurt
2 teaspoons vanilla extract
200ml vegetable oil

For the sandwich icing:
100g milk chocolate
300g butter, softened
450g icing sugar
50g cocoa powder
100g caramel

CONTINUED OVERLEAF

For some of these recipes, I'd created names for them before coming up with the actual end product and this was one of them. It was one of the last recipes I did as I couldn't decide what I wanted to create for the ultimate celebration cake. When I finally had the idea it was like a light bulb had gone off in my head. I wanted it to be huge, chocolatey and decadent, with a towering chocolate feast on top. A real showstopper. I thought Mars bars with a classic chocolate butter cream would taste amazing, however, because the Mars bars and icing just wouldn't combine, I ended up stirring melted chocolate and caramel into buttercream to create that same Mars bar taste. I think this is such a special cake and I urge you to make it for someone celebrating something really exciting.

· · · · · · · · · · · · ·

Preheat the oven to 180°C/350°F/GM4. Grease and line the cake tins.

Put the milk, treacle and chocolate in a saucepan and stir over a low heat until melted and combined. Set aside until needed.

Put the flour, sugar, cocoa powder, baking powder and bicarbonate of soda in a large mixing bowl.

Whisk in the eggs, Greek yoghurt, vanilla extract and oil, then stir in the chocolate mix until smooth and well combined.

Divide the mixture between the cake tins and bake for 20 minutes, until risen and springy to touch. Transfer to a wire rack and allow to cool completely in the tins.

RECIPE CONTINUES OVERLEAF

For the ganache:
100ml double cream
200g dark chocolate
  (70% cocoa solids)

To decorate:
4 Mars bars
50g honeycomb
edible gold glitter
sparklers

Now make the icing. Melt the chocolate in a bowl set over a pan of simmering water, making sure the bottom of the bowl doesn't touch the water, then set aside to cool slightly.

In a bowl, cream the butter and slowly add the icing sugar and cocoa until smooth, light and fully incorporated. Stir through the melted chocolate and caramel to form a smooth icing.

To make the ganache, warm the cream over a low heat until bubbles form at the side of the pan, then take off the heat and add the chocolate. Stir until melted – if your ganache mixture is looking too stiff, or is breaking slightly, you can add a little warm milk to loosen it and reach the desired consistency. Set aside to cool.

Now assemble the cake. Sandwich the cakes together with a layer of icing, then spread the icing over the top and sides until nice and smooth.

Pour the cooled ganache on top of the cake and ease it over the sides to create drips.

Cut the Mars bars and honeycomb into shards and dust with glitter. Stick in some sparklers and serve!

# TOP TEN BAKING MEMORIES

*(hopefully you can add to this as you bake from this book either if you're relaxed and happy from baking solo, or having fun with a friend or family member )*

-----------------------------------------

-----------------------------------------

-----------------------------------------

-----------------------------------------

-----------------------------------------

-----------------------------------------

-----------------------------------------

-----------------------------------------

-----------------------------------------

-----------------------------------------

-----------------------------------------

-----------------------------------------

-----------------------------------------

-----------------------------------------

-----------------------------------------

-----------------------------------------

-----------------------------------------

-----------------------------------------

# NOTES

# INDEX

## A

almonds
    Amazing Chocolate
        Brownies 74
    Flourless Coconut
        & Lime Cake 100
    Granola 196
    Peanut Butter Cups 54
    Plum & Almond Cake 111
    Raspberry & Lemon
        Friands 44
Amazing Chocolate
    Brownies 74
American Stack Pancakes
    204
apple
    Apple & Blackberry
        Crumble 142
    Nanny's Apple Pie 150
    Tarte Tatin 158
Apple & Blackberry
    Crumble 142
Australian Toasted Banana
    Bread 108
Autumn Pavlova 136
avocado
    Amazing Chocolate
        Brownies 74

## B

Baileys Tiramisu 126
banana
    Australian Toasted
        Banana Bread 108

Jim's Mum's Banoffee
    Pie 122
Birthday Cake 237
Birthday Cupcakes 238
Biscotti, Cranberry,
    Pistachio & Chocolate 19
biscuits
    Custard Creams 22
    Edible Christmas Tree
        Decorations 221
    Mary Berry's Chocolate
        Fork 24
    Skeleton 225
    Vanilla & Pistachio 20
    White Chocolate &
        Nutella Pinwheel 27
blackberries
    Apple & Blackberry
        Crumble 142
    Autumn Pavlova 136
blueberries
    Blueberry Muffins 50
    French Toast 200
Blueberry Muffins 50
Bread & Butter Pudding,
    Marmalade 134
Brownie Cake 103
brownies
    Amazing Chocolate 74
    Salted Caramel 57
buns
    Cinnamon 176
    Hot Cross 230
    Iced 184
    Nutella 182

buttermilk
    Blueberry Muffins 50
    Chocolate Fudge Spider-
        web Cake 226
    Peaches & Cream Muffins
        46
    Pretty Yellow Big Easter
        Cake 234
    Rhubarb & Custard
        Muffins 60

## C

cake pops: Pumpkin Pops
    222
Cappuccino Cake 84
caramel
    Choc. Honeycomb
        Caramel Cupcakes 58
    Jim's Mum's Banoffee Pie
        122
    Millionaires' Shortbread
        64
    Salted Caramel Brownies
        57
    Salted Caramel
        Cheesecake 125
    Ultimate Celebration Cake
        241–2
Carrot Cake 104
Cheat's Croissants 199
cheese, cream
    Carrot Cake 104
    Cheesecake & Dark Choc.
        Cupcakes 73

Chocolate Orange
    Cheesecake 141
Pumpkin Pops 222
Pumpkin Whoopie Pies 70
Salted Caramel
    Cheesecake 125
cheese, mascarpone
    Baileys Tiramisu 126
    French Toast 200
Cheese Scones 181
Cheesecake & Dark Choc.
    Cupcakes 73
cheesecakes
    Chocolate Orange 141
    Salted Caramel 127
Cherry Bundt Cake 98
Choc Chip Shortbread 15
chocolate
    Amazing Chocolate
        Brownies 74
    Baileys Tiramisu 126
    Brownie Cake 103
    Cheesecake & Dark Choc.
        Cupcakes 73
    Choc Chip Shortbread 15
    Choc. H'comb Caramel
        Cupcakes 58
    Chocolate Fudge Spider-
        web Cake 226
    Chocolate Loaf 91
    Chocolate Orange
        Cheesecake 141
    Cornflake Choc Chip
        Cookies 33
    Cranberry, Pistachio &
        Choc. Biscotti 19
    Easter Nests 233
    Festive Yule Log 212

Halloween Cupcakes 228
Jim's Mum's Banoffee Pie
    122
Maddie's Mum's Choc.
    Roulade 138
Mary Berry's Choc. Fork
    Biscuits 24
Milk & White Chocolate
    Cookies 37
Millionaires' Shortbread
    64
Mini Chocolate Cookies
    16
Mocha Cake 97
Nigella's Cookie Dough
    Pots 144
Pain au Chocolat 199
Peanut Butter & Dark
    Choc. Cookies 30
Peanut Butter Cups 54
Profiteroles 164
Rocky Road 49
Salted Caramel Brownies
    57
Salted Chocolate Tart
    166
Salted Chocolate Truffles
    218
Skeleton Biscuits 225
S'mores Cupcakes 62
Sunday Cake 87
Super Duper Chocolate
    Cake 118
Triple Chocolate Cookies
    38
Ultimate Celebration
    Cake 241–2
*see also* white chocolate

Chocolate Fork Biscuits,
    Mary Berry's 24
Chocolate Fudge Spider-
    web Cake 226
Chocolate Honeycomb
    Caramel Cupcakes 58
Chocolate Loaf 91
Chocolate Orange
    Cheesecake 141
Christmas Tree
    Decorations, Edible
    221
cinnamon
    Cinnamon Buns 176
    Oat & Cinnamon Healthy
        Cookies 34
Cinnamon Buns 176
coconut
    Flourless Coconut &
        Lime Cake 100
    Kate's Mum's Lemon
        Slice 67
coconut oil
    Amazing Chocolate
        Brownies 74
    Granola 196
    Peanut Butter & Dark
        Choc. Cookies 30
    Peanut Butter Cups 54
coconut sugar
    Amazing Chocolate
        Brownies 74
    Peanut Butter & Dark
        Choc. Cookies 30
coffee
    Baileys Tiramisu 126
    Cappuccino Cake 84
    Mocha Cake 97

condensed milk
   Kate's Mum's Lemon
      Slice  67
   Millionaires' Shortbread
      64
Cookie Dough Pots,
   Nigella's  144
cookies
   Cornflake Choc Chip  33
   Milk & White Chocolate  37
   Mini Chocolate  16
   Oat & Cinnamon Healthy
      34
   Peanut Butter & Dark
      Chocolate  30
   Reindeer  215
   Salted Nutella  28
   Triple Chocolate  38
Cornflake Choc Chip
   Cookies  33
Cranberry, Pistachio &
   Chocolate Biscotti  19
Croissants, Cheat's  199
Crumpets  207
cupcakes
   Birthday  238
   Cheesecake & Dark
      Chocolate  73
   Chocolate Honeycomb
      Caramel  58
   Halloween  228
   Raspberry  53
   S'mores  62
   Vanilla Star-sprinkled  79
   *see also* muffins; small
      cakes
custard
   Custard Creams  22

Custard Tarts  156
   Rhubarb & Custard
      Muffins  60
   Strawberry Tarts  155
Custard Creams  22
Custard Tarts  156

**D**

Doughnuts  175
dried fruit
   Earl Grey Tea Loaf  88
   Fruit Scones  178
   Hot Cross Buns  230
   *see also* raisins

**E**

Earl Grey Tea Loaf  88
Easter Nests  233
Edible Christmas Tree
   Decorations  221

**F**

Festive Yule Log  212
Flapjacks, Smarties  68
Flourless Coconut & Lime
   Cake  100
French Toast  200
Friands, Raspberry &
   Lemon  44
fruit cakes: Earl Grey Tea
   Loaf  88
Fruit Scones  178
Frying Pan Pizza  187

**G**

Gingerbread Loaf  112
Granola  196

**H**

Halloween Cupcakes  228
hazelnuts
   Autumn Pavlova  136
   Nutella Buns  182
honey
   Granola  196
   Oat & Cinnamon Healthy
      Cookies  34
Hot Cross Buns  230

**I**

Iced Buns  184

**J**

Jamie Oliver's American
   Stack Pancakes  204
Jim's Mum's Banoffee
   Pie  122

**K**

Kate's Mum's Lemon
   Slice  67

**L**

large cakes
   Birthday  237
   Brownie  103
   Cappuccino  84

Carrot 104
Cherry Bundt 98
Chocolate Fudge Spider-
        web 226
Festive Yule Log 212
Flourless Coconut &
        Lime 100
Mocha 97
Pineapple Upside-down
        133
Pistachio Cake with
        Lemon Curd 94
Plum & Almond 111
Pretty Yellow Big Easter
        234
Rainbow 106
Sunday 87
Super Duper Chocolate 118
Ultimate Celebration
        241–2
Victoria Sponge 115
see also loaf cakes
lemon
        Autumn Pavlova 136
        Kate's Mum's Lemon
                Slice 67
        Lemon Drizzle Loaf 92
        Lemon Meringue Pie 129
        Lemon Tart 152
        Pistachio Cake with
                Lemon Curd 94
        Raspberry & Lemon
                Friands 44
Lemon Drizzle Loaf 92
Lemon Meringue Pie 129
Lemon Tart 152
Lime Cake, Flourless
        Coconut & 100

loaf cakes
        Australian Toasted
                Banana Bread 108
        Chocolate 91
        Earl Grey Tea 88
        Gingerbread 112
        Lemon Drizzle 92


M
Maddie's Mum's Chocolate
        Roulade 138
maple syrup: Peanut Butter
        Cups 54
Marmalade Bread & Butter
        Pudding 134
marshmallow
        Rice Krispie Squares 76
        Rocky Road 49
        S'mores Cupcakes 62
Marshmallow Rice Krispie
        Squares 76
Mary Berry's Chocolate
        Fork Biscuits 24
mascarpone cheese
        Baileys Tiramisu 126
        French Toast 200
meringue
        Autumn Pavlova 136
        Lemon Meringue Pie 129
Milk & White Chocolate
        Cookies 37
Millionaires' Shortbread 64
Mince Pies 216
Mini Chocolate Cookies 16
Mocha Cake 97
muffins
        Blueberry 50

Peaches & Cream 46
Rhubarb & Custard 60
see also cupcakes; small
        cakes


N
Nanny's Apple Pie 150
Nigella's Cookie Dough
        Pots 144
Nutella Buns 182
Nutella Cookies, Salted 28
White Chocolate & Nutella
        Pinwheel Biscuits 27


O
Oat & Cinnamon Healthy
        Cookies 34
oats
        Granola 196
        Oat & Cinnamon Healthy
                Cookies 34
        Smarties Flapjacks 68
orange
        Chocolate Orange
                Cheesecake 141
        Marmalade Bread &
                Butter Pudding 134


P
Pain au Chocolat 199
pancakes
        Crepes 194
        Jamie Oliver's American
                Stack 204
Pancakes 194

Pavlova, Autumn 136
Peaches & Cream Muffins 46
Peanut Butter & Dark
    Chocolate Cookies 30
Peanut Butter Cups 54
pear: Autumn Pavlova 136
pecan nuts
    Pecan Pie 162
Pecan Pie 162
pies
    Jim's Mum's Banoffee
      122
    Lemon Meringue 129
    Mince 216
    Nanny's Apple 150
    Pecan 162
    Pumpkin 161
    *see also* tarts
Pineapple Upside-down
    Cake 133
Pistachio Cake with Lemon
    Curd 94
pistachio nuts
    Cranberry, Pistachio &
      Choc. Biscotti 19
    Pistachio Cake with
      Lemon Curd 94
    Vanilla & Pistachio
      Biscuits 20
Pizza, Frying Pan 187
Plum & Almond Cake 111
Pop-Tarts 202
Pretty Yellow Big Easter
    Cake 234
Pretzels 172
Profiteroles 164

puff pastry
    Cheat's Croissants 199
    Custard Tarts 156
    Pain au Chocolat 199
    Tarte Tatin 158
Pumpkin Pie 161
Pumpkin Pops 222
Pumpkin Whoopie
    Pies 70


R

Rainbow Cake 106
raisins
    Carrot Cake 104
    Cinnamon Buns 176
    Hot Cross Buns 230
    Oat & Cinnamon Healthy
      Cookies 34
    Peanut Butter & Dark
      Choc. Cookies 30
    *see also* dried fruit
raspberries
    French Toast 200
    Raspberry & Lemon
      Friands 44
    Raspberry Cupcakes
      53
Raspberry & Lemon
    Friands 44
Raspberry Cupcakes 53
Reindeer Cookies 215
Rhubarb & Custard
    Muffins 60
Rocky Road 49
Roulade, Chocolate 138

S

Salted Caramel Brownies 57
Salted Caramel Cheesecake
    125
Salted Chocolate Tart 166
Salted Chocolate Truffles 218
Salted Nutella Cookies 28
scones
    Cheese 181
    Fruit 178
shortbread
    Choc Chip 15
    Millionaires' 64
shredded wheat: Easter
    Nests 233
Skeleton Biscuits 225
small cakes
    Easter Nests 233
    Peanut Butter Cups 54
    Pumpkin Pops 222
    Pumpkin Whoopie Pies 70
    Raspberry & Lemon
      Friands 44
    *see also* cupcakes; muffins;
      traybakes
Smarties Flapjacks 68
S'mores Cupcakes 62
Sticky Toffee Pudding 130
strawberries
    Strawberry Tarts 155
    Victoria Sponge Cake 115
Strawberry Tarts 155
sultanas: Carrot Cake 104
    *see also* dried fruit; raisins
Sunday Cake 87
Super Duper Chocolate
    Cake 118

**T**

Tarte Tatin 158
tarts
    Custard 156
    Lemon 152
    Pop-Tarts 202
    Salted Chocolate 166
    Strawberry 155
    Tarte Tatin 158
    *see also* pies
tea
    Autumn Pavlova 136
    Earl Grey Tea Loaf 88
Tiramisu, Baileys 126
tomato: Frying Pan Pizza
    187
traybakes
    Amazing Chocolate
        Brownies 74
    Kate's Mum's Lemon
        Slice 67
    Marshmallow Rice
        Krispie Squares 76
    Millionaires' Shortbread 64
    Rocky Road 49
    Salted Caramel Brownies
        57
    Smarties Flapjacks 68
Triple Chocolate Cookies 38
Truffles, Salted Chocolate
    218

**U**

Ultimate Celebration Cake
    241–2

**V**

Vanilla & Pistachio Biscuits
    20
Vanilla Star-sprinkled
    Cupcakes 79
Victoria Sponge Cake 115

**W**

Waffles 192
white chocolate
    Choc Chip Shortbread 15
    Chocolate Loaf 91
    Milk & White Chocolate
        Cookies 37
    Nigella's Cookie Dough
        Pots 144
    White Chocolate &
        Nutella Pinwheel
        Biscuits 27
    Pretty Yellow Big Easter
        Cake 234
    Pumpkin Pops 222
Whoopie Pies, Pumpkin 70

**Y**

yoghurt
    Super Duper Chocolate
        Cake 118
    Ultimate Celebration
        Cake 241–2
Yule Log, Festive 212

## ACKNOWLEDGEMENTS

I have lots of thank yous to give:

To my wonderful team Dom, Lucy, Kate and Georgia for showing me enormous amounts of support, enthusiasm and dedication as we continue on this crazy journey.

To the brilliant people who all had a part in making this book with me. Fenella, Emma, Tamara, Charlie, Emily, Nicola, Poppy, Susanna, Olivia, Dan, Sam, Adam and Annie. I couldn't have wished for more passionate and fun people to work with on this book.

To the unbelievably supportive, kind and lovely people who watch my videos and read my blog for their constant loyalty. I love you guys.

To my friends and family for always being there for me to give me advice and to those who shared their incredible recipes with me and allowed me to then share them with the world.

And of course to Jim, thank you for always believing in me and being my chief taste taster!